HARRY KIRKE WOLFE

Ludy T. Benjamin, Jr.

HARRY KIRKE WOLFE
Pioneer in Psychology

University of Nebraska Press

Lincoln and London

The paper in this book meets
the minimum requirements of
American National Standard for
Information Sciences—Permanence
of Paper for Printed
Library Materials, ANSI z39.48–1984.

Benjamin, Ludy T., 1945–
  Harry Kirke Wolfe: pioneer in
  psychology / Ludy T. Benjamin, Jr.
      p.   cm.
  Includes bibliographical references.
  ISBN 0-8032-1196-1 (alk. paper)
  1. Wolfe, Harry Kirke. 2. Psychologists—
  Nebraska—History. 3. College
  teachers—Nebraska—History.
  I. Title.
  BF109.W64B45   1991
  150'.92—dc20
  [B]   90–34206
  CIP

This book is dedicated to
    Isabel Wolfe Hemenway
    Katharine Alice Wolfe
    Harry Kirke Wolfe II

Contents

Preface

When Harry Kirke Wolfe began his college studies in 1876, the seeds of the science of psychology were in their final minutes of germination, a centuries-long germination that began when humans first pondered the nature of their existence. The soil of the "old psychology" of the rationalists, the mentalists, and the associationists was about to give birth to the "new psychology" of the psychophysicists, the physiologists, and the experimentalists. Mutations of the philosophical psychology of Aristotle, Descartes, and Locke would bring forth the experimental psychology of Fechner, Wundt, and Ebbinghaus. Wolfe was a witness to the emergence of this new psychology. Captivated by its promise, he transplanted the German cuttings to Nebraskan soil, nurturing their growth.

Wolfe studied at two German universities with two of the new psychology's most distinguished pioneers, one of whom, Wilhelm Wundt, had founded the world's first psychological laboratory at Leipzig in 1879 during Wolfe's senior year at the University of Nebraska. Studying at that laboratory, Wolfe became one of the first two Americans to earn a psychology degree there. He then returned to his adopted state of Nebraska, where he established one of America's earliest psychology laboratories.

As a member of the founding generation of American psychology, Wolfe has been largely forgotten while many of his contemporaries comprise the personal histories of American psychology as written today. One of the purposes of this book is to show that this is an obscurity that is undeserved.

Chiefly this is a book about Wolfe as a psychologist and

teacher. His life and career are described in the socio-political context of Nebraska and its newly founded state university and against the intellectual background of an emerging American experimental psychology. The book is a case history in the struggles of the psychological laboratory and the controversies surrounding the applications of the new psychology. It is an account of the politics of education. However, it is ultimately the story of a professor of psychology who was arguably the most inspiring teacher of his generation.

My initial contact with Wolfe's name came in 1970, my first year of college teaching, when I was preparing lectures for a course in the history of psychology, which I was teaching at Nebraska Wesleyan University in Lincoln. In one of the textbooks I was reading was a listing of Wundt's American doctoral students and the psychology laboratories they founded. At the bottom of the list was "H. K. Wolfe—Nebraska." Had I been teaching in another state, I would likely have overlooked his name. Clearly the word *Nebraska* caught my attention; yet, I was also intrigued by the fact that Wolfe's name was the one name that I did not recognize.

My curiosity led me to search the published sources in the history of psychology, looking for information on Wolfe. I thought some history of local origin would especially interest my students, most of whom were Nebraska natives. Principally my goal was to use what I found for my lectures, and like all new teachers, I was desperately in need of lecture material. I soon learned that there was *no* published information about Wolfe but that there were some unpublished documents written by him and about him in the archives of the University of Nebraska. It was the beginning of a search that continues to this day.

The more I learned about Wolfe, the more interested I became in his character and in his contributions as an educator. The search led me from archive to archive and eventually to the storehouse of records and memories of his children. After twenty years of searching and reading, the puzzle of Wolfe's life is still incomplete, as all biographies are; there are many gaps in the archival record, particularly in terms of personal correspondence. Yet much richness of material remains.

This book is not a psychological biography, although speculations about motive, personality, and social process appear occasionally. Instead, it is chiefly a chronological account in narrative style, drawn principally from archival records and oral histories and, to a lesser extent, from published materials.

In writing this book, I do not intend to argue that Wolfe deserves inclusion on American psychology's Mount Rushmore alongside the likenesses of William James, G. Stanley Hall, James McKeen Cattell, or John B. Watson. He was no match for them as theoretician, writer, researcher, organizer, or entrepreneur for the discipline of psychology. Instead he substantially influenced psychology as a teacher, indirectly through the contributions of his many students. Those contributions merit more than the mere listing of his name among Wundt's American students. It is my hope that this book adequately conveys the life of this selfless man and his important legacy for American psychology.

Ludy T. Benjamin, Jr.
Texas A & M University

Acknowledgments

A project of twenty years' duration owes a debt of gratitude to a great many individuals. I gratefully acknowledge their assistance in making this book a reality.

Henryk Misiak and Virginia Staudt Sexton introduced me to H. K. Wolfe by listing his name in their 1966 book, *History of Psychology: An Overview,* a book that also helped me to have something to say in my first semester of teaching.

Clifford L. Fawl, my department chair at Nebraska Wesleyan University, fostered my development as a college professor, supported my growing interest in the history of psychology, and encouraged my research and writing on Wolfe. He remains an important mentor to me and is a close friend. Had they been contemporaries, he and Wolfe would have been good friends.

Amy D. Bertelson, now a clinical psychologist at Washington University in St. Louis, was the first undergraduate student to work with me on Wolfe and was the coauthor of the first article I published about him. She has continued her interest in the history of psychology and in this book.

John A. Popplestone and Marion White McPherson, the directors of the Archives of the History of American Psychology at the University of Akron, have supported my efforts as a historian of psychology for fifteen years. All of psychology owes them a considerable debt for their establishment of "The" archives, and like most of my published work, this book draws on the richness of the Akron collection.

Richard Dienstbier and Herbert Howe, as the chairs of the Department of Psychology at the University of Nebraska, have been most encouraging of my work on Wolfe and have partially supported it with funds for the archival research.

Joseph G. Svoboda, the long-time archivist for the University of Nebraska, has been assisting my work, off and on, for nearly twenty years. His knowledge of the contents of the archival collections at the university and his willingness to help are appreciated.

Joseph McVicker Hunt is Professor Emeritus of Psychology at the University of Illinois and a 1929 baccalaureate graduate of the University of Nebraska. His father was one of Wolfe's students. Joe encouraged me to write a biography of Wolfe long before I was convinced that such a book was possible, and he has prodded me repeatedly over the years to complete it.

Michael M. Sokal, a historian of science at Worcester Polytechnic Institute, the Executive Secretary of the History of Science Society, and a friend, has been of immeasurable help in my work for the past fifteen years. His scholarly writing on James McKeen Cattell is an ideal to which I aspire.

A number of archives have made available to me materials that have been used to write this book: Archives of the History of American Psychology, University of Akron; Clark University (Stuart W. Campbell, Archivist); Cornell University; Library of Congress, Manuscript Collections; Nebraska State Historical Society; University of California-Berkeley, Bancroft Library; University of Iowa; University of Nebraska-Lincoln, Love Library; and University of Michigan, Michigan Historical Collections, Bentley Historical Library. I am grateful for their assistance and for permission to quote from their materials.

A portion of one chapter in this book is drawn from a book chapter I wrote with Emily S. Davidson, my colleague at Texas A&M University. The book was published by Plenum Press. I am grateful to both for permission to use that work here.

I also want to express my appreciation to Sydney Ellen Schultz, who prepared the index for this book.

Texas A&M University provided some grant funds in support of the research for this book and, most important, a sabbatical leave to complete the writing. I am especially thankful to Stephen Worchel, my department chair, for helping me to secure the sabbatical.

Several students—Lenora McKeen, Jodi Hauptman, and Cathy Grover—have assisted my research in important ways, handling requests on short notice, always with eagerness and good cheer. They were captured by Wolfe's magic as a teacher and perhaps count themselves among his students.

Linda Hosea and Wendy Shlossman transcribed more than fourteen hours of taped interviews I conducted with Wolfe's two daughters and son. Both performed extremely well on a difficult task.

My colleague and friend Jack R. Nation has supported this project in several ways. Of greatest importance was his handling of the myriad of production and publication details on the revision of our introductory psychology textbook and, by doing that, allowing me the freedom to work on the Wolfe manuscript almost uninterrupted.

Over the years, a number of my colleagues, some of whom have been mentioned already, have helped me in my understanding of Wolfe and the historical context of which he was a part. That kind of help has also come from my students, many of whom share with me a passion for the history of psychology.

My wife, Priscilla, and our two daughters, Melissa and Melanie, have known Wolfe as a household word for many years. They have shared in the joy of this project and understand, probably better than anyone else, its importance to me.

The Wolfe family has been particularly supportive of this book. This includes Wolfe's daughter-in-law, Pearl Wolfe; two of his grandsons, Arthur Hemenway, who made many helpful suggestions on an earlier draft of this book, and Kirke Wolfe; and a granddaughter, Jan Hemenway Carpenter. Special thanks go to Jann McFarland, Wolfe's great-granddaughter, and her husband, Sid, for their help in reproducing many of Wolfe's papers that are part of the family archives. The many hours they spent at the copy machine are greatly appreciated.

My greatest debt is to the Wolfe "children," whom I first met in 1981: Isabel Wolfe Hemenway (1889–1987), Katharine Alice Wolfe, and Harry Kirke Wolfe II. They welcomed me into their homes, participated in hours of interviews, and made available to me their father's existing papers: a large collection of notebooks from his study in Germany, class lectures, scrapbooks of newspaper clippings, and some correspondence. Harry was particularly helpful in answering many written queries and in commenting on earlier drafts of the book. This book clearly could not have been written without the help of these three special people. Like their father, they have spent much of their lives helping others. It is to them that this book is dedicated.

Chapter One

The Making
of a Teacher

Credit for the founding of psychology as an experimental science, independent of philosophy, is typically accorded to Wilhelm Maximilian Wundt (1832–1920), who in 1879 initiated a program of psychological research in his laboratory at the University of Leipzig.[1]

The American Psychological Association in 1979 celebrated the centennial of that accomplishment by minting a silver medallion featuring Wundt's face on the obverse. The following year, the Twenty-second International Congress of Psychology, which now convenes every four years, met in Leipzig in celebration of the Wundt centenary. Among the special events at the congress was the issuing of a Meissen porcelain medallion picturing Wundt in profile on the obverse.

Although this new science took root and initially flourished in European soil, an early wave of American students was soon busy transporting it across the Atlantic to America's fledgling universities. There it would enjoy unparalleled success, with American psychology laboratories quickly dotting the country. Forty had been established by 1900, only seventeen years after the first American psychology laboratory was founded at Johns Hopkins University.[2] By the 1920s, American universities, which still played second fiddle to their European counterparts in the older physical and biological sciences, could claim preeminence in the science of psychology.

In fact, the 1920s were a time of enormous popularity for American psychology. The new experimental scientists found themselves much in demand, prompting the Canadian humorist Stephen Leacock to lament that America was suffering from an "outbreak of psychology."[3] Indeed, much of the American public seemed convinced that the science of psychology held the keys to individual prosperity and happiness. A daily newspaper columnist observed in 1928:

> Men and women never needed psychology so much as they need it to-day. Young men and women need it in order to measure their own mental traits and capacities with a view to choosing their careers early and wisely . . . businessmen need it to help them select employees; parents and educators need it as an aid in rearing and educating children; all need it in order to secure the highest effectiveness and happiness. You cannot achieve these things in full measure without the new knowledge of your own mind and personality that the psychologists have given us.[4]

The pinnacle of American psychology's success in the 1920s was marked in 1929 by the Ninth International Congress of Psychology, which met on the campus of Yale University. It was the fortieth anniversary of the international congresses, which normally were held every three to four years, and it was the first of the psychology congresses to be held in North America. American psychologists had attempted to host the congress in 1913, but petty squabbling and a power struggle within the American ranks prevented its occurrence.[5] No psychology congresses met during World War I, and in the years immediately following the war, economic conditions in Europe made attendance at an American meeting impossible.[6]

However, in the first week of September 1929, more than one hundred foreign psychologists were gathered in New Haven, Connecticut, with more than seven hundred of their American contemporaries. The week-long meeting was a showcase of American psychology, long awaited by James McKeen Cattell

(1860–1944), one of its founders and the man elected by his colleagues to serve as president of the ninth congress. Cattell opened the congress with a formal address entitled "Psychology in America." He traced the brief history of American psychologists and remarked, "In the production of psychologists the universities of Indiana and Nebraska stand high."[7]

That remark was based on two surveys conducted in the 1920s by a University of Pennsylvania psychologist, Samuel Fernberger. Surveying the entire membership of the American Psychological Association, a chiefly scientific organization founded in 1892, Fernberger analyzed the undergraduate backgrounds of its members as an indicator of sources of inspiration for psychology. He wrote that he found it "curious" that the University of Nebraska ranked third, in both surveys, in the production of students who would go on for doctoral study and a career in psychology.[8]

Nebraska's ranking was more than curious; it was remarkable. How was it possible that a primarily agricultural institution, founded as recently as 1869, could compete so successfully with the more prestigious universities of the East? American psychology was synonymous with Harvard, Cornell, Columbia, Clark, Johns Hopkins, and Yale. The eastern universities had more extensive libraries, better-equipped psychology laboratories, notable doctoral programs, large psychology faculties, and outstanding students. For most of the first half-century of American psychology, the University of Nebraska had no graduate psychology program, meager laboratory facilities, and typically only one or two faculty members teaching psychology at any one time. How was it that in those fifty years the University of Nebraska was able to surpass most other institutions as a nursery for psychologists? The answer is, of course, the subject of this book.

Harry Kirke Wolfe (1858–1918) was one of Wilhelm Wundt's American doctoral psychology students, who numbered just more than a dozen, and in contemporary histories of psychology, he is among the least known of that group.[9] After his study in Germany, Wolfe returned to his alma mater, the University of Nebraska, where in 1889 he founded one of the earliest American psychology laboratories, possibly the first that was devoted exclusively to the training of undergraduate students. Except for a nine-year period, he remained a faculty member at Nebraska for the rest of his life.

Wolfe was one of thirty-one charter members of the American Psychological Association, yet he never held an elected office in that organization. He was associated with the founding of the first American psychology journal (the *American Journal of Psychology*), yet he published only a couple of articles in its pages. While his contemporaries parlayed their degrees in the new psychology into fame and places in the history books, Wolfe returned to Nebraska and obscurity.

Although Wolfe achieved little fame for himself, his students numbered among the most eminent psychologists of their generation, with three of them being elected to the presidency of the American Psychological Association. They were part of the score of psychologists in the 1920s whose inspiration for the field came from their undergraduate classes with Wolfe. His special commitment to students is a prominent theme in this book.

Wolfe's parents were Jacob Vance Wolfe and Eliza Ellen Batterton, both natives of Indiana. Jacob Wolfe was born October 7, 1833, in Merom, Indiana, a small town perched on a bluff overlooking the Wabash River. His childhood was spent on a farm near Merom, where he attended a rural school. In 1850, his family moved to Bloomington, where he enrolled in the preparatory academy of the state university and two years later in the university proper. He graduated with a baccalaureate in the classics in 1857 and secured a teaching position at Glendale Women's College in Glendale, Ohio, near Cincinnati. There he met Ellen Batterton, also a member of the faculty and a teacher of mathematics.

Ellen Batterton was a native of Bloomington, Indiana. Born on September 20, 1836, she was educated in Bloomington's schools. She had hoped to attend Indiana University; however, women were barred from enrollment there, so she attended the Monroe County Female Seminary, also in Bloomington, and graduated with a degree in mathematics. For a couple of years she taught in the public schools of Bloomington before being elected to the chair in mathematics at Glendale.

Jacob Vance and Ellen Batterton Wolfe

Jacob and Ellen were married at Glendale College on December 18, 1857, with the president of the college, J. G. Montfort, presiding at the ceremony. The Wolfes finished the 1857–58 school year at Glendale and then moved to Bloomington, Illinois. It was there that their first child, Harry Kirke Wolfe, was born on November 10, 1858.

Jacob Wolfe taught for several years in Illinois and in Gosport, Indiana, where a daughter, Nellie Batterton Wolfe, was born in 1861. After the family moved to Bloomington, Indiana, Wolfe entered the law school of Indiana University. A second son, Frank, was born during this time. Jacob Wolfe received his law degree in 1863 and established his legal practice in Spencer, Indiana, about fifteen miles northwest of Bloomington. For nine years the family resided in Spencer, where three more of the Wolfe children were born: Miriam, Jessie, and Jacob Vance, Jr. Frank died shortly before his first birthday, and Miriam lived only about seventeen months.

Jacob Wolfe's interests soon turned to politics; he served a term in the Indiana legislature and two terms as Owen County treasurer for the Democratic party. In 1871, at age thirty-eight and at the close of his second term as treasurer, he decided to visit Lincoln, Nebraska, apparently on a whim. Interviewed years later by a newspaper reporter on the occasion of his fiftieth wedding anniversary, he reminisced about that decision.

Just why I came, I am myself sometimes at a loss to know. One reason that might seem sufficient, was that at that time Indiana had plenty of good men, and especially good democrats to spare, for the woods were just full of them. . . . My coming was merely accidental if not providential. . . . Visiting Indianapolis one day I saw numerous large posters headed in large letters: "To Lincoln, Nebraska, and return. Only $20." I immediately made up my mind that a trip like that was what I wanted and needed.[10]

Jacob Wolfe liked what he saw: wide-open spaces and new opportunities. He bought a farm south of Lincoln, in the community of Normal, one mile east of the state penitentiary. After a brief return to Indiana to settle family affairs, he brought his wife and four children to the Nebraska farm in April 1872.

For many years Jacob Wolfe was content to farm, returning to the occupation of his youth and a life he had enjoyed. Spring was his favorite season and he delighted in the changes it brought forth, both in nature and in the plowed fields. The farm was a good place for a family to be, and in the Wolfes' first five years in Nebraska, the final three of their nine children were born: Mary, William, and Paul.[11]

Because both Jacob and Ellen were former college teachers, it is not surprising that education was stressed in the Wolfe home. Ellen Wolfe had given up her teaching job when her first child was born; however, she continued her own education as a voracious reader—a "lover of books."[12] Apparently she infected her children with her interest in books and her love of learning. Six of the seven children who reached adulthood would graduate from the University of Nebraska, and the seventh, Mary, would complete the two years of college then required for a teaching certificate.

Harry Kirke Wolfe was thirteen when the family moved to the farm near Lincoln. As the eldest of the children, he had considerable responsibility for the work of the farm. He shared his mother's love of books, so much so that he read while walking behind the plow, learning Latin from Julius Caesar's *Gallic War*.[13] After a combination of education at rural schools, at home, and behind the plow, Wolfe, at the age of sixteen, entered the preparatory academy of the fledgling University of Nebraska.

When Jacob Wolfe had visited Lincoln in 1871, University Hall, the first building of the University of Nebraska, had just opened. It was a structure built amid much controversy over Nebraska's need for an institution of higher education. Some believed that the building, whose foundation began to crack and crumble even before it was occupied, was a three-story omen for the future of higher education in Nebraska.

Interest in higher education had existed since Nebraska's establishment as a territory in 1854, and several private colleges had been founded. In 1869, two years after Nebraska attained statehood, the charter for the university was approved by the legislature in a bill that called for the establishment of a "State Lunatic Asylum and University and Agricultural College" in Lincoln. The language of the bill was later altered by amendment to make it clear that the state university and the state lunatic asylum were to be separate institutions.[14]

Classes began at the university in September 1871 with an enrollment of about 130 students. Only about twenty of those took college classes; the remainder enrolled in the preparatory academy. The first two students graduated from the university in 1873, and by 1876, the year Wolfe began his college work, ten students had earned their baccalaureate degrees. When Wolfe arrived, the university was truly in its infancy. There was still considerable public controversy about the university, including the argument that it was an extravagance the state could ill afford. Controversy also existed within the campus as the chancellor, regents, faculty, and students pressed their often disparate ideas about the nature of the university. Conflicts ranged from the expansion of the university's curriculum in medicine, agriculture, and engineering to the establishment of compulsory chapel and military drill, to the place of religious instruction in the university.[15]

Education at the university was composed of the classics—Greek, Latin, mathematics, and philosophy—a curriculum that had been standard fare in American universities before the Civil War. Based on the educational theory of the day, a theory drawn from Scottish faculty psychology, these subjects were of critical importance because they provided mental discipline. It was believed that appropriate study could strengthen the faculties of the mind, just as strenuous exercise could strengthen the muscles of the body. This curriculum of mental discipline, according to Jeremiah Day, the president of Yale University in the early 1800s, was

> best calculated to teach the act of fixing the attention; directing the train of thought; analyzing a subject proposed for investigation; following with accurate discrimination the course of argument; balancing nicely the evidence presented to the judgment; awakening, elevating, and controlling the imagination; arranging, with skill, the treasures which memory gathers; rousing and guiding the power of genius.[16]

Physical science was often absent from the curriculum, and when it existed, it was without laboratory training. Although this remained the case at the University of Nebraska, many other American universities changed their curricula after the Civil War, when American educational reformers called for a more elective curriculum with classes in laboratory science and with opportunities for students' involvement in original research. This new curriculum was modeled after that of the German universities and pioneered by the University of Berlin.

But when Wolfe began his college work in 1876, he entered an inflexible course of study in the classical tradition. The transcript for his first year of college lists classes in Greek, geometry, algebra, and botany.[17] His best grade was in the botany class. As a sophomore he took a second year of Greek; a year of Latin; another year of math with classes in trigonometry, analytic geometry, and calculus; and classes in chemistry and rhetoric. His focus on the classics emulated the educational preparation of his father and the mental-discipline curriculum of old. However, there were no other choices.

A notation on Wolfe's transcript for 1877–78 indicates he was "exempt from military drill." Since the beginning of classes at the university, some officials had worried aloud that the university was not in compliance with one of the provisions of the Morrill Act, which had established the university as a land-grant college. The federal gift of ninety thousand acres of land to the university, as an endowment and in support of an agricultural college, required that military training be offered to all male students. Such drill was not initiated until 1876 when an army lieutenant recently graduated from West Point joined the Nebraska faculty. At first the military training was voluntary. However, in December 1876, the regents passed a resolution requiring uniforms for drill, and at their summer meeting in June 1877, they made military drill compulsory for all male students.

A number of students were troubled by the new requirements, and a series of secret meetings was held in the fall term of 1877. A petition was signed by nineteen male students asking the university for exemption from drill because they could not afford to purchase the required uniforms. Wolfe's classmate, Howard Caldwell, was among the signers, and it is likely, although not certain, that Wolfe signed the petition as well. In recalling their action, Caldwell wrote, "The answer was awaited in trembling expectancy for the brave nineteen had resolved to go to some other school rather than to submit to such tyranny."[18] The university responded that uniforms would not be required for the current academic year because an announcement had not been made in a timely fashion. There were to be two drill units, one with uniforms and one without. The latter unit became known as the "ragamuffin squad." The students agreed they had been outflanked by the university's officials, and most drilled.

The university's chancellor, Edmund B. Fairfield, was not enamored with compulsory military training and was a reluctant supporter. Some said he was too reluctant, because he gave exemptions to virtually any student who requested one, regardless of the legitimacy of the student's request. Eventually this issue was one of several that led to Fairfield's dismissal in 1882.[19] Wolfe's reason for exemption is not known; however, according to his university transcript, he was excused for two of his four years.

In his third year, Wolfe continued his program of study in the classics, with a year of Greek literature, a year of language study in German, a year of physics, and other classes in English literature, logic, and European history. Some of his grades during his first and second years had been in the average range, particularly for the math and chemistry courses. But as a junior he improved his scores markedly, and as a senior he earned nine As and three Bs in his twelve courses.

Wolfe's senior-year curriculum was more diverse than his earlier years of study but was still largely prescribed by the university.[20] He took a year of science, with classes in geology, zoology, and meteorology; two classes in American government; two in literature; one in international law; and another in political economy. One other course that Wolfe took would have ties to his eventual career choice of psychology: a year-long class in mental and moral philosophy, a course required of all seniors.

Such courses were common in the latter half of the nineteenth century; typically they were taught by college presidents whose background was in the clergy. At Nebraska that instructor was Chancellor Fairfield, a former Baptist minister. These courses, which represented American psychology before the "new psychology" of William James (1842–1910), were based on the Scottish mental philosophy of Thomas Reid, John Witherspoon, and Dugald Stewart. In America, the Scottish school, the "old psychology," was perhaps best represented by James McCosh and Noah Porter, both presidents of American universities, the former at Princeton and the latter at Yale.[21] Both had written important textbooks on psychology as the science that could reveal the soul, and Porter's works were used in the course at Nebraska.[22]

According to one historian of psychology, Thomas Leahey, courses in mental philosophy were "installed as a safeguard against what religious leaders took to be the skeptical and atheistic tendencies of British empiricism."[23] Taught as psychology, these courses represented a final attempt to ensure

Harry Kirke Wolfe (ca. 1880)

morality in the brightest of America's youth. And many college presidents saw that as one of their important duties.

In the fall of his senior year, Wolfe reached the age of twenty-one, and a Lincoln newspaper carried an account of the surprise birthday party given for him, now that he was "at that age, fixed by law, when boys become men." His classmates arrived at his parents' house on a cold and rainy evening and found Wolfe "totally absorbed in his lessons."

After numerous slices of conversation, sandwiched with music, Mr. Mercer, One of Mr. W.'s classmates, arose in all his native modesty, and after paying a handsome tribute, . . . said to the hero of the evening, "As a slight testimonial of the esteem in which you are held by your classmates, I have the pleasure, in their name, of presenting to you this beautiful edition of 'Hume's History of England,' and . . . I present you this elegant gold pen and pencil, hoping that, with this pen, you may write your name higher up on the scroll of literary fame than the author of these volumes ever dreamed of."[24]

We are told that Wolfe was apparently genuinely surprised but rallied with appropriate remarks of gratitude for the tokens of esteem from his friends. David Hume's history thus became an early acquisition in the substantial library that Wolfe accumulated over the course of his life. Indeed, his book buying would become something of an addiction.

Wolfe's senior class consisted of seven men and one woman, the largest graduating class to that date. They gathered on the morning of June 9, 1880, at the Lincoln Opera House for the commencement ceremonies. As was the custom, each of the graduates, in alphabetical order, gave a brief speech. Wolfe would have been last except for his classmate J. H. Worley. Bouquets of flowers were thrown on the stage after each speech as Chancellor Fairfield awarded the degrees.

Wolfe's address, like the others, was discussed in the newspapers.

"Philosophy and Christianity" was Mr. Wolfe's subject, and most philosophically was it written. We think his production was one of the best, both in thought and style of composition that was delivered. It evinced careful study and close application of fact.[25]

Another newspaper, noting that Wolfe's address was "listened to with marked attention," provided a brief summary of the message. That summary provides a glimpse of Wolfe's philosophy of science at age twenty-one and is important in understanding his later work in the science of psychology.

Science, philosophy, and religion comprehend all that man has ever known, thought, or hoped, said the speaker. Science is given all praise, merely for reaping the harvest sown by other hands. Philosophy is regarded with little favor, while religion grows stronger. Christianity, rejected by the Jews, was joyously received by the Greeks and Romans. The reason of this is to be determined by a study of their previous thought. The last conversation of Socrates demonstrates the ability of the human reason to solve the problem of man's existence, and to satisfy his longing for the unseen. Previous to his time the struggle of the Grecian mind for truth was in vain. The results were materialism and skepticism. Socrates introduced the

subjective method (of study) and urged all to a study of
self. A rational psychology resulted. If it is possible for human reason to discover the nature of the soul, it can only
be done by analyzing the manifestations of the soul. Socrates then adopted the proper method, his conclusions
were imperfect, because inductive reasoning requires a
multitude of facts, and he had collected comparatively
few, yet he died a believer in one God and in the soul's
immortality. . . .

Greek philosophy divinely appointed or otherwise, was
the preparatory school for Christianity. . . . Philosophy
has accomplished a noble work; but it is said that she has
perished, and that science occupies her throne, explaining
what she could not understand, walking where she could
not penetrate. But science can only accumulate facts. Philosophy must use them. She is queen leading the world to
truth. Science is her chief engineer, subordinate, and sub-
servient. Philosophy moves, not in a circle, but in a spiral,
around an inverted cone, and as she rises we hear her ever
exclaiming, "Why, whence and whither art thou, oh,
man!"[26]

It is possible, perhaps probable, that the subject of the address was chosen because of the religious debates that were
prominent on campus during Wolfe's student years. In his history of the University of Nebraska, Robert Manley has written,
"During the first years of the institution no single topic was
more discussed than the proper relation of religion to higher
education."[27] These "religious wars" had cost the university's
first chancellor, Allen R. Benton, his job and were a strong factor in the dismissal of Chancellor Fairfield.

By the fall of 1879, the religious controversy was at its ze-
nith. Some people argued that religion was too prominent on
the campus, while others bemoaned its absence. Compulsory
chapel and the religious nature of those services were topics of
continued debate. There was also concern about the religious
affiliations of the faculty. Some of the populace called for diversity so that no particular denomination would be in control;
others, the Methodists for example, argued for a faculty of
their own religious persuasion. Certain professors were at-

tacked for failing to teach Christian principles in their classes. And particular classes were criticized for teaching the ideas of atheists.[28] Wolfe's talk certainly addressed this last point.

Wolfe was not an especially religious person. In that respect he was similar to his father, who was described as having a simple faith based in Christian principles. Jacob Wolfe was a man of high integrity and one who showed a great tolerance for the beliefs of others. His son espoused a similar philosophy and was rarely involved in organized religion, although, as an adult, he did attend the Unitarian Church on a sporadic basis.

Although Wolfe was not religious, he was intrigued by theological questions and the potential for philosophical inquiry in learning the nature of the soul—the goal of a rational psychology. The concept of a rational psychology that he used in his commencement address came from Christian von Wolff (1679–1754), a German philosopher who spent most of his life at the University of Halle. Christian von Wolff's two most important books were *Empirical Psychology* (1732) and *Rational Psychology* (1734). The former was a psychology of the person, based on the knowledge of experience; the latter was a psychology of the soul, based on the processes of reason. Empirical psychology was subject to illusions and tricks of sensation and, as such, was much less reliable than rational psychology.[29] Despite Wolfe's apparent fervor, at the age of twenty-one, for a rational psychology, he would later reject that for the promise of the new psychology, a science grounded in the tenets of empiricism.

Wolfe and his classmates, whose career plans were announced at the commencement exercises, were divided between careers in law (3) and teaching (4) The eighth graduate, J. H. Worley, did not indicate his career goals. Howard Caldwell intended to be a teacher, as did Emma Parks, the one female member of the class. David Mercer, who had presented the gifts at Wolfe's surprise birthday party, planned to become a lawyer. Not surprisingly, Wolfe announced that he would pursue a career as a teacher.[30]

Hanging above the commencement stage was a large white muslin banner, lettered in green: *"Palma non sine pulvere"*— "There are no wreaths without conflict." It was an interesting class motto, given that three of the eight classmates would be embroiled thirty-eight years later in the greatest conflict in the history of the university, one that provided no wreaths for any of its participants.

In the fall of 1880, Wolfe began a series of three public school jobs as principal and teacher, first at Park School, a ward school in Lincoln; second at Ponca, Nebraska; and third at Edgar, Nebraska, a small town about ninety miles southwest of Lincoln. He was well liked in Edgar, as indicated by a number of glowing letters from school board members attesting to his performance. However, having taught for three years, he decided to pursue graduate study in the classics. He was especially interested in philosophy, which was not surprising, given the nature of his graduation address.

Although he could have chosen to study in several graduate programs in the United States, Wolfe elected instead to continue his education at the University of Berlin, a university that had been much discussed in American educational circles because of its curricular innovations. Graduate education was still a small enterprise in America. It is estimated that at the time Wolfe went to Germany, the number of Americans pursuing graduate study abroad equaled the number similarly engaged at home.

In Berlin, Wolfe would pursue his doctorate in the classics, intending to return as a teacher in a college or university. His experience in Berlin would not change his occupational goal, but it would radically alter his intended field of study. It would change his views on science and on the viability of a rational psychology, offering him the chance to train in the newest of the sciences—the new psychology.

Chapter Two

Germany and
the New Psychology

Pursuit of advanced study in European universities has been characteristic of American students since the birth of the United States. Although there were undoubtedly many reasons for this intellectual migration, one broad appeal of such study was an exposure to the art, music, architecture, and history of many centuries. In short, European study afforded a cultural richness that was synonymous with being "well educated."

With the beginning of the nineteenth century, Americans migrating to Europe for study increasingly chose German universities. The prestigious universities at Heidelberg, Leipzig, and Göttingen were several hundred years old when the University of Berlin, founded in 1809, advanced its philosophy of *Wissenschaft*, thus changing the face of university education. This philosophy promoted an active epistemology, particularly with regard to science, and a freedom of teaching and inquiry that had not been characteristic of universities. The University of Berlin established well-equipped laboratories, where professors were encouraged to conduct research and to involve their advanced students in that work, teaching them the methods of original inquiry. Professors were given a great deal of freedom to teach what they wished and to research questions of their own choosing. *Wissenschaft* also extended to the curriculum: students were given considerable freedom in selecting courses toward their degrees.[1]

This change in the nature of the university was radical; likely it could have occurred only at a new institution such as the University of Berlin. Soon, other German universities adopted a similar model; as a result, Germany would achieve international prominence in science and preeminence in the fields of chemistry, physics, and medicine by the end of the nineteenth century. The attraction of study in Germany is evidenced by the estimated fifteen thousand Americans who studied medicine there between 1870 and 1914.[2]

The beginnings of laboratory science in American universities lagged behind Germany by about forty years; laboratories in physics and chemistry were founded in the 1840s.[3] Most of these early laboratories were established by Americans who had taken their advanced study in Germany. That pattern was repeated for the founding of American psychology laboratories at the end of the nineteenth century.

As part of this student migration, Wolfe arrived in Berlin in October 1883, not to pursue scientific study but to earn a doctorate in the classics. Whatever his savings might have been from his three years of teaching, they were not enough to support his study abroad. He received a number of loans from his family, the first in August 1883 (one hundred dollars) and the second (eighty dollars) soon after his arrival in Berlin. In early November, a week before his twenty-fifth birthday, Wolfe registered for his first-semester classes at the University of Berlin. His courses were typical of a graduate program in the classics: Greek city-states, Greek mythology, the history of philosophy, and Roman history.[4]

Little is known of Wolfe's activities during his almost three years in Germany. With no existing correspondence from his German study, the written record consists of his class notes, recorded in the paper-covered booklets (*Hefte*) popular with German students, and a small ledger. The ledger lists the loans he received, the books he purchased, and the theater, opera, and concerts he attended. For his stay in Berlin he listed nine

Page from Wolfe's registration book for his second semester (1884) at the University of Berlin listing the two psychology courses of Hermann Ebbinghaus

performances, including three Shakespearean plays: *Hamlet, Romeo and Juliet,* and *The Merry Wives of Windsor.*[5]

Wolfe's study of the classics continued in the second semester with courses on Plato, logic, the Greek language, and literary and historical criticism. In addition, he took two other courses that would change his life, one entitled "Psychology" and the other "Fundamentals of Experimental Psychology."[6] Both classes were taught by a thirty-four-year-old instructor, Hermann Ebbinghaus (1850–1909).

Ebbinghaus had received his doctorate in philosophy from the University of Bonn in 1873. Five years later he began his now famous studies on memory, presenting that research in 1880 to the faculty at Berlin as his *Habilitationsschrift*, the second thesis that was necessary to become a university professor. It was accepted, and Ebbinghaus began teaching at the University of Berlin; however, his position was that of a *Privatdozent*, an unsalaried lecturer.[7]

Around the time of Wolfe's arrival in Berlin, Ebbinghaus resumed his studies on memory. He first replicated his earlier experiments, comparing the results, and then extended his work to other factors in memory. These studies were published in 1885 in Ebbinghaus's most famous book, *Über das Gedächtnis* (*On Memory*), indisputably one of the classics of modern psychology.[8]

Influenced by Gustav Fechner's (1801–87) experimental investigations of sensation, described in his book on psychophysics,[9] Ebbinghaus set out to apply the experimental method to the study of the higher mental processes of learning and memory. Unlike the British empiricists, who had used a kind of retrospective analysis to study associations that were already formed, Ebbinghaus wanted to study the actual formation of associations and their subsequent retention. One of the problems he faced was that for a literate person, words have meaning and thus already possess many associations. How was he to eliminate the confounding variable of prior associations? His pondering of that question led to one of the great insights in the history of experimental psychology: Ebbinghaus's invention of *sinnlose Silben*, literally translated as "meaningless syllables" and today referred to in psychology as "nonsense syllables." One author has suggested that Ebbinghaus may have gotten the idea for nonsense syllables from reading Lewis Carroll's poem *Jabberwocky* during an 1876 visit to London.[10]

Ebbinghaus generated twenty-three hundred of these three-letter syllables by creating all possible letter combinations in a consonant-vowel-consonant arrangement. Each syllable was lettered on a card; stimulus materials for each of his studies were then randomly selected from the set of cards. Edward Bradford Titchener (1867–1927), one of the most famous

know of Wundt before he came to Germany, he did learn about him in Ebbinghaus's courses, as recorded in his class notes.

The most plausible reason for Wolfe's departure from Berlin hinges on Ebbinghaus's faculty status. As a *Privatdozent*, Ebbinghaus lacked professorial rank and thus was incapable of supervising Wolfe's doctoral work. Because Wolfe had decided to abandon his pursuit of the classics and devote himself to the new psychology, he had to go elsewhere to earn his doctorate. What better place than the most famous of psychology laboratories?[19]

When Wolfe arrived in Leipzig in 1884 there were two other American students studying with Wundt. One was James Thompson Bixby, a Unitarian minister who was studying philosophy. Bixby's dissertation on Herbert Spencer's ethics was completed in 1885, earning him the distinction of being the first of Wundt's American doctoral students.[20] However, he was not a psychology student. The other American was James McKeen Cattell, the twenty-four-year-old son of the president of Pennsylvania's Lafayette College. Cattell had arrived in Leipzig around the time Wolfe had begun his study in Berlin.

Wolfe and Cattell began fall-term classes toward the end of October, with Wolfe enrolling in Wundt's very crowded psychology course. Cattell, who decided to attend few of the lectures in his second year, described the psychology classroom in a letter to his parents. "The air is so bad, as to be really injurious. In Prof. Wundt's lecture room there are packed some three hundred men—the ceiling is low and not a crack is left open."[21] The heavy enrollment, even with the bad air, evidenced the popularity of Wundt and his subject matter.

Wundt graduated from the University of Heidelberg in 1855, finishing at the top of his medical school class. After a short time in Berlin, where he worked with Johannes Müller (1801–58), Wundt returned to Heidelberg to work as an assistant to Hermann von Helmholtz (1821–94).[22] There he published his first book, on muscular movements and sensations, in 1858. A second book, *Contributions to the Theory of Sensory Perception*, followed in 1862. It was in this book that Wundt laid out his plans for psychology, an experimental science that would uncover the facts of consciousness. At this time he was teaching a course on experimental physiology, in which he included some psychological material. By 1867 the title of Wundt's course had become "Physiological Psychology," and out of these lectures emerged his most important work, *Principles of Physiological Psychology* (1873–74). This book went through six editions in Wundt's lifetime and is clearly among the most important publications in the history of psychology. It was a compendium of all the research related to Wundt's vision of an experimental psychology. In the preface to the work Wundt stated his purpose clearly, noting that it was his intention to establish psychology as a new domain of science. It was an act of scientific courage and considerable vision.[23]

In 1874, Wundt took a position at Zurich University, but he stayed there only a year before accepting a newly established professorship in philosophy at the University of Leipzig. There he would remain for the rest of his life, establishing the first psychological laboratory at the age of forty-seven and, two years later in 1881, the first psychological journal, *Philosophische Studien*. It was the beginning of an academic Mecca that drew students from all over Europe and from the United States and Canada. In his career, Wundt directed the doctoral theses of sixty-six psychology students, most of them from Germany and Austria. Although approximately forty Americans studied with Wundt in Leipzig, only thirteen of those completed their doctorates in psychology with him: Cattell was the first, Wolfe was the second.[24]

For Wundt, psychology was the study of *immediate experience*, that is, experience devoid of any cultural, social, or linguistic interpretations. The more biased experience was called *mediate experience*, meaning it was mediated by the processes of learning. Immediate experience was basic, unfettered by learning; this was the experience Wundt sought to study. His research used a laboratory setting to create experiences that could be repeated, that could be independently verified by others, and that were thus subject to systematic study. The principal method of study in Wundt's laboratory was introspection, an experimental form of self-observation. In employing this technique, Wundt laid down explicit criteria for its use, including the requirement that stimulus variables be altered in various trials to discover how such manipulations affected the subject's experience. Introspective judgments were primarily quantitative in nature, and dealt mostly with sensory dimensions such as intensity and duration.[25] Other methods were also used, including the psychophysical techniques of Fechner and certain physiological procedures. Wolfe wrote of Wundt, "Gradually he has won the psychological students to his methods, which are after all merely the methods of the other sciences."[26]

Judging from the dissertation topics and the publications in Wundt's journal, nearly 70 percent of the research of the Leipzig laboratory concerned sensation and perception. This majority reflected the empirical emphasis on the senses as the conduit for learning, as well as the important nineteenth-century work in sensory physiology by Müller, Helmholtz, and others. Other Leipzig studies involved reaction time, emotion, learning (association), and attention.[27]

Having defined the subject matter of psychology as the study of immediate experience, Wundt stated the goal of psychology to be the analysis of experience into its component elements: sensations and feelings. This atomistic approach sought to reduce experience to its most basic elements. However, Wundt's plan was more than just the delineation of a psychological periodic table. In addition to determining what constitutes an element of experience, he was also interested in discovering how these basic elements combine to create what he called "psychical compounds." This process, according to Wundt, occurred through "creative synthesis," producing new qualities not inherent in the basic elements. "It is a general principle valid for all psychical compounds, whether they are composed of sensations only, of feelings only, or of combinations of both sensations and feelings, that the attributes of psychical compounds are never limited to those of the elements that enter into them."[28]

In the early years of the Leipzig laboratory, Wundt was active in supervising the work of his doctoral students, often numbering around a dozen in residence each year. After the turn of the century, that yearly average was sometimes as large as twenty-five; however, much of the work was handled by Wundt's assistants, while he devoted more time to his writing.

Wundt has been characterized in psychological histories as an autocratic individual who did not tolerate opinions that differed from his own. He is said to have assigned research problems to his students, allowing them no choice in the matter. Although such histories are colorful and fit the stereotype of the German *Herr Geheimrat Professor*, they are not generally supported by the available evidence. Cattell, writing as a student at Leipzig, told his parents he had a great deal of freedom in selecting his research topics. Wolfe's dissertation topic, the only one on memory in the first thirteen years of Wundt's laboratory, also suggests that students had a say in their work. Reminiscences from other students characterize Wundt as supportive of his students, open to change in his ideas when given evidence that he was wrong, and kind in his interactions with them, inviting them to Sunday suppers at his home. There are incidents in these reminiscences of dogmatism on Wundt's part, but they seem to be the exception rather than the rule.[29]

Wundt was an exceptionally popular lecturer, certainly one of the most popular at the University of Leipzig. His classes were always taught in the largest classroom on campus; because every seat was typically occupied, some students almost always had to stand. In his later years his class was moved to a new auditorium with five hundred seats, and still it was oversubscribed.[30] His students were impressed by his erudition, indeed by his encyclopedic knowledge of so many subjects. In his years at Leipzig, Wundt taught thirty-two different courses, principally in philosophy and psychology but also a few in anthropology and physics.[31]

Students also praised Wundt's lectures for their clarity, their conclusiveness, and their inherent synthesis and analysis. According to one student, his lectures may have been too complete in that they left little unanswered for the students, thus not stimulating independent thought.[32] Wundt spoke slowly, with precise enunciation, and was enthusiastic about his subject, particularly his experimental demonstrations. One image of Wundt as lecturer is provided in a letter written by Edward Bradford Titchener in 1890 after attending his first class with the fifty-eight-year-old Wundt.

Wilhelm Wundt (Photo courtesy of the Archives of the History of American Psychology)

The *famulus* swung the door open, and Wundt came in. All in black, of course, from boots to necktie; a spare, narrow-shouldered figure, stooping a little from the hips; he gave the impression of height, though I doubt if in fact he stands more than 5 ft. 9.

He clattered—there is no other word for it—up the side-aisle and up the steps of the platform: slam bang, slam bang, as if his soles were made of wood. There was something positively undignified to me about this stamping clatter.

He came to the platform, and I could get a good view of him. Hair iron-grey . . . Eyes dark behind rather small-glassed spectacles, very good, honest, friendly, alert. . . .

The platform has a long desk, I suppose for demonstrations, and on that an adjustable book-rest. Wundt made a couple of mannered movements,—snatched his forefinger across his forehead, arranged his chalk—and then faced his audience with both elbows set on this rest. A curious attitude, which favours the impression of height. He began his lecture in a high-pitched, weak, almost apologetic voice; but after a sentence or two, during which the room settled down to silence, his full lecturing voice came out, and was maintained to the end of the hour. It is an easy and abundant bass . . . it carried well, and there is a certain persuasiveness, a sort of fervour, in the delivery that holds your interest and prevents any feeling of monotony. . . . Wundt, so far as I could tell, never looked down once at the book-rest, though he had some little shuffle of papers there between his elbows. . . .

Wundt did not keep his arms lying on the rest: the elbows were fixed, but the arms and hands were perpetually coming up, pointing and waving. . . . I had the fanciful impression that Wundt was using his hands where the ordinary lecturer turns his head and eyes; the movements were subdued, and seemed in some mysterious way to be illustrative. Very characteristic, anyhow, the rigid body and the almost rigid head, and these hands playing back and forth between the voice and the audience.

He stopped punctually at the stroke of the clock, and clattered out, stooping a little, as he had clattered in. If it wasn't for this absurd clatter I should have nothing but admiration for the whole proceeding.[33]

Wundt often worked at home in the mornings, reading, working on his journal, and writing. In early afternoon he came to the laboratory, where he would attend examinations, make his rounds of the laboratory projects, and meet with students. His classes were always in the late afternoon, typically at four, which meant that during the Leipzig winters, they began in darkness.

In the years when Cattell and Wolfe were in residence at Leipzig, there was a special excitement about the promise of the new science and a recognition of the pioneering nature of the work being done in the laboratory. These sentiments are expressed in a letter Cattell wrote to his parents in January 1884.

> Our work is interesting. If I should explain it to you you might not find it of vast importance, but we discover new facts and must ourselves invent the methods we use. We work in a new field, where others will follow us, who must use or correct our results. We are trying to measure the time it takes to perform the simplest mental acts—as for example to distinguish whether a color is blue or red. As this time seems to be not more than one hundredth of a second, you can imagine this is no easy task.[34]

Wolfe was not involved as a researcher in this mental chronometry work, although he did serve Cattell as a subject in those studies.[35] In fact, the record provides no indication of what research, if any, Wolfe was conducting during his initial year at Leipzig.

Wolfe's class notes indicate that his course load for the fall 1884 semester consisted of a psychology class from Wundt, a class in pedagogical psychology from Ludwig Strumpell, and classes in ethics and Greek culture. The following year he took three more courses from Wundt: a second one on ethics, one on logic, and another on the history of modern philosophy. He was also preparing for the secondary fields, archeology and ancient cultures, to be covered in his doctoral exams, and he took at least three courses on those subjects.

Despite the press of his classes and, in 1885, the development of his dissertation research, Wolfe continued to indulge his interests in opera, theater, and ballet. He was especially fond of Richard Wagner (who died the year Wolfe arrived in Berlin) and collected Wagner records most of his life. His ledger lists thirty-six performances he attended during the two years he spent in Leipzig, including *Faust, Carmen, Antigone, Fidelio, Orpheus of the Underworld, The Marriage of Figaro, Cosi fan Tutte, Tristan und Isolde,* and *Lohengrin.* Several productions he saw a second time, including Wagner's comedy *Die Meistersinger von Nürnberg, Hamlet,* and a performance of *Romeo and Juliet* in Dresden.[36]

As noted earlier, memory, Shakespeare's "warder of the brain," was to become the subject of Wolfe's dissertation. It was the first dissertation on memory by one of Wundt's students; subsequently there were two others, one in 1899 and another in 1912.[37] In the twenty-three years that Wundt edited his journal (1881–1903), he published only six articles whose principal concern was memory. The rarity of these studies at Leipzig stemmed from Wundt's belief that experimental methods could not be used to investigate higher mental processes such as memory. Ebbinghaus's successful investigations did little to change Wundt's mind on this question. In the 1903 edition of his *Principles of Physiological Psychology,* Wundt did acknowledge Ebbinghaus's studies on memory as important, but added that the research was preliminary.[38] Despite these feelings, Wundt permitted Wolfe to investigate this topic in the Leipzig laboratory and to use that work for his doctorate.

Ebbinghaus, although influenced by Fechner's use of the scientific method to study the processes of sensation, had not used psychophysical methods in his investigations of memory. That was largely because Ebbinghaus studied retention by the method of recall, or what he called "reproduction." Wolfe chose instead to investigate retention by the method of recognition, a method that requires a stimulus to be present and the subject to make a judgment about the stimulus. This paradigm lends itself well to psychophysical methods, particularly the method of constant stimuli, which was the method Wolfe used in his research on the memory for tones.[39] Wolfe believed recognition memory was a simpler and more basic kind of memory process that recognized objects or events as familiar or unfamiliar. Its fundamental nature made it a building block for understanding more complex memory abilities.

In early 1885, Wolfe began collecting the extant references on memory in philosophy and psychology, dating to Plato's ideas.[40] Ebbinghaus's book appeared that year and is frequently cited in the published version of Wolfe's dissertation. Further, Ebbinghaus's studies are acknowledged to be the impetus for the problem Wolfe chose to research. Why Wolfe chose to study auditory memory is not clear; most of the sensory studies at Leipzig involved investigations of vision. One very reasonable hypothesis, considering the time of the research, was that tone stimuli were selected because of the important book on the psychology of tone published by Carl Stumpf (1848–1936) in 1883. Yet Stumpf's book is not noted in Wolfe's dissertation. Instead, in reference to audition, Wolfe cites the much earlier work of Helmholtz.[41]

Wolfe's research involved the presentation of two tones in succession, each having a duration of one second. The interval between the offset of the first tone and the onset of the second tone was varied from 1 second to 120 seconds. The task of the subject was to say whether the second tone was the same or different in pitch and, if different, whether it was higher or lower. Tones were generated by a series of three hundred tuning forks across a five-octave range from 32 to 1,024 cycles per second. The study was repeated with a second group of subjects selected according to their musical abilities and classified as either "musical" or "unmusical."[42]

The principal finding of the studies was that the longer the interval between the two tones, the less it was likely that the second tone would be correctly identified. And like the course of forgetting described by Ebbinghaus, Wolfe found that most forgetting took place rapidly and then tapered off as the interval increased. Within the tone range investigated, Wolfe found that high tones were more accurately recognized than low tones. Further, the unmusical subjects were prone to judge the high tones as too high and the low ones as too low when compared with the more musically sophisticated subjects.[43]

The research was reviewed in two American journals, *Science* (1886) and the *American Journal of Psychology* (1887), by Joseph Jastrow (1863–1944), who had recently received his doctorate in psychology from G. Stanley Hall (1844–1924), at Johns Hopkins University. Some of Jastrow's comments were positive; for example, the review in *Science* began, "A very interesting study is that on the 'Memory for Tone' by Mr. H. K. Wolfe." But then Jastrow criticized the studies, arguing that they were seriously flawed because the use of response categories by the subjects made the data open to ambiguous interpretations.[44] He was right with regard to the first study, but in the second study the response categories were changed. The interpretation of common conditions in the two studies is virtually the same, suggesting that Jastrow's concern was not well founded.

Wundt added the results of Wolfe's studies to the discussion of memory in the next edition of his *Principles of Physiological Psychology* (1887), and William James gave Wolfe's research a full page in his *Principles of Psychology* (1890). In a section entitled "Exact Measurements of Memory," James discusses the work of only two individuals: Ebbinghaus and Wolfe. Neither James nor Wundt mentioned Jastrow's criticisms.[45] Certainly Wolfe was aware of Jastrow's reviews. What impact they had on him is not known; however, their nature is such that he must have been disappointed, if not hurt. He did not respond to Jastrow's methodological charges.

The dissertation study marked the end of Wolfe's research in memory, perhaps as a result of the negative reaction the studies received from Jastrow. In addition, Wolfe's study did not generate much of a follow-up at Leipzig. Another memory study, similar in design but using color tints instead of tones, was conducted in 1886 by Alfred Lehmann, a Danish psychologist who was a postdoctoral student with Wundt. Lehmann had been one of the subjects for Wolfe's research. Yet memory studies remained a rarity, and thirteen years passed before another dissertation study on memory was conducted in Wundt's laboratory. Commenting on Wundt's research agenda, the psychologist and historian Edwin G. Boring has written, "Wundt went his own way, and his laboratory with him, and outside discoveries did not greatly deflect his course."[46]

Instead, memory became the province of the psychology laboratory at Göttingen where Georg Elias Müller (1850–1934) began his work in 1887 with his assistant Friedrich Schumann (1863–1940).[47] Their work, and the earlier studies by Ebbinghaus, dominated the scientific literature on memory into the twentieth century; in contrast, Wolfe's study, although cited in detail by James, was rarely mentioned. This point is clear in Boring's summary of the research projects emanating from Wundt's laboratory. "The other studies on tonal memory, recognition practice, mediate association, and the course of association (1886–1901) made little impression as compared with the effective research upon memory by Ebbinghaus and G. E. Müller that belongs to the same period."[48]

Wolfe passed his doctoral exams in the spring of 1886 and, perhaps in celebration, took a brief vacation in Italy. Cattell too was in Italy, and he wrote his parents from Rome about his chance meeting with Wolfe. "Here I meet people I know, among them a man Wolfe, whom I have mentioned in my letters. He is quite an able fellow, made his examination at the same time I did, and with a psychological thesis. He has studied art and archeology (the latter one of his subjects in the examination) so it is pleasant for us to go to the museums and galleries together and discuss matters."[49]

Wolfe defended his doctoral thesis on August 17, 1886. He returned to Nebraska at the end of the summer with no immediate job prospects, although he hoped to secure a university philosophy chair. In November he received a letter Wundt had written for Wolfe's use in his job search.

Mr. H. K. Wolfe has been in attendance for several semesters at the University of Leipzig during which time he has attended my lectures and was an active participant in the work of my psychological seminary. I have learned to know him as a well informed conscientious and diligent man.

He has proved himself especially capable of conducting psychological investigations and, I doubt not, will prove himself in the future. I am convinced therefore that Mr. Wolfe's talents and attainments make him thoroughly competent to fill a position as teacher of psychology, especially so to an introduction of students into experimental psychology.[50]

There was no open position in philosophy at the University of Nebraska, and for a year Wolfe was unemployed. In the summer of 1887 he learned of and applied for a philosophy-psychology position at the University of Wisconsin. Several of his former professors from the University of Nebraska wrote letters supporting him. At the same time he applied for public school jobs as a principal or superintendent, in Nebraska and elsewhere.[51] He did not get the job at Wisconsin; ironically, that position was filled by Joseph Jastrow. However, through the assistance of a family friend he was offered a position as principal of the high school in San Luis Obispo, California, where he began work in the fall of 1887.

Katharine Brandt Wolfe (ca. 1890)

Living in a boarding house in San Luis Obispo, Wolfe met a young female physician, Katharine Hermine Brandt, who was working in the charity program of the local Catholic mission. Charity work was common for female physicians in the nineteenth century; establishing a paying practice was difficult because customers, both women and men, frequently had doubts about the competence of women as doctors. Brandt had moved to California in November 1887 from her hometown of Philadelphia after graduating with her medical degree from the Women's Medical College of Pennsylvania in April of that year.

Brandt was born August 7, 1865, in Pennsylvania of German immigrant parents. Her father, Herman Brandt, had left Germany in 1846 at the age of thirteen because his family had sought to avoid conscription of their sons. Taught by a private tutor, Katharine Brandt received all of her schooling at home because of her "delicate" nature: both her hearing and her vision were thought to be deficient. To aid her hearing, her ears were pierced when she was eight, and later her four eyeteeth were pulled in the belief that the procedure would improve her eyesight. She grew up speaking both German and French, the latter because of her Alsatian maternal grandmother who lived with the Brandts. A special tutor was hired to prepare Brandt for medical school.[52]

In medical school Brandt became close friends with Isabel Cowie, an older woman. One year behind Brandt in the college, Cowie was the daughter of a British army colonel assigned to Calcutta. The two spoke often about practicing medicine together after graduation, deciding on an exotic life in India treating the Muslim and Hindu women who, wearing the purdah, could not be thoroughly examined by male physicians. But Harry Wolfe, who was very much taken with Katharine, hoped to change those plans.

In the fall of 1888, in his second year as principal, Wolfe received an invitation from the University of Nebraska to assume the chair in philosophy beginning in September 1889. Brandt knew it was the job he wanted more than any other. He told her he would not accept the job offer unless she agreed to marry him. Likely his "threat" played no role in her decision, but she did accept his offer. They were married December 16, 1888, in San Francisco in a brief ceremony witnessed by two of Brandt's brothers who were California residents. Wolfe, who was never fond of jewelry, reluctantly purchased a wedding band for his wife, referring to it as a "symbol of barbarism."[53]

The two Dr. Wolfes finished their respective duties in the spring, enjoying their new life together. Harry, eager to return to Nebraska, began working on the lectures he would deliver in his fall classes, including a new offering at the university— "Psychology." Three years after leaving Leipzig, Wolfe was about to test Wundt's assessment of him as a teacher of psychology.

Chapter Three

Mental States
and Sugar Beets

The Wolfes arrived in Lincoln in the summer of 1889; Katharine was pregnant with their first child, Isabel. For a time they stayed with Wolfe's parents on the farm in Normal, but then moved to a rented apartment in the Lincoln business district, near the university. It was the first of many housing moves that became an almost annual event for the Wolfes.

The university had changed little since Wolfe's graduation in 1880. The enrollment of 317 students at that time had grown to 384 students by the beginning of the fall term in 1889. Although the growth of the university had been slow during the 1880s, that rate did not mirror the dramatic increase in the population of Nebraska, which rose from an 1880 census figure of approximately 450,000 to over 1,060,000 in 1890.

The Nebraska historian James Olson has called the 1880s "years of progress and prosperity" in Nebraska. Rainfall was excellent during much of the decade, especially in the central regions of the state, where the new settlers flocked to establish their farms. By the end of the decade, food production and the number of livestock on farms had tripled. The cities also fared well, as manufactured goods increased 700 percent during the decade. Omaha's population growth reflects these trends, mushrooming from thirty thousand in 1880 to approximately one hundred thousand in 1890. Yet the boom came to an abrupt end at the close of the decade because of overspeculation by banks, dramatically falling farm prices, and one of the most disastrous blizzards in the nation's history.[1]

The 1890s began with a continuation of the economic slide of the late 1880s. Severe drought, the worst in twenty-five years, foretold hard times for the state. Indeed, after the doubling of the population in the 1880s, the growth in the 1890s was a mere four thousand, an increase of less than a half-percent. Paradoxically, the university's growth for the 1890s would be more than five-fold. With problems on the land, the sons and daughters of farmers came to the university in ever larger numbers, staking their claims to their parents' dreams of a better life.

The university had long acknowledged its role of service to the farmers of the state and clearly recognized the long-term economic realities of its dependence on agricultural prosperity. Motivated in part by that dependence and by a desire to fulfill the obligations of the Morrill Act, the university opened the College of Agriculture in 1872. Its establishment was greeted by Nebraska's farmers with emotions ranging from suspicion to outright disdain. They were not interested in being told how to farm by professors who had never walked behind a plow. And many laughed at the idea that the agricultural graduates, the "book farmers," would be able to make a living from the land. However, those attitudes began to change in the late 1880s, partly because of the efforts of Charles Bessey (1845–1915).

Bessey, a renowned botanist and specialist on Nebraska plant life, became acting chancellor of the university in 1888. A strong supporter of agricultural education, he sought to recruit would-be farmers to the university. In 1889 he wrote a series of articles for the *Nebraska Farmer*, arguing that the changing complexity of farming necessitated a university education for success in agriculture. Perhaps because of the positive reception of his message, the university's classes began to swell. Enrollment for 1890 was 570, an increase of 48 percent over the previous year, and in the next five years it increased to more than 1,500 students.[2]

Wolfe could not have imagined the growth his university was

about to undergo when Bessey invited him to join the faculty as Lecturer in Philosophy. He was hired as head of the philosophy department, a dubious honor because he was the only faculty member in the department. But it was *the* position he had longed for—his alma mater, his adopted state, his chance to teach the new psychology. He wasted no time in pressing his interests in scientific psychology and education, two areas that were certainly not traditional offerings in philosophy curricula.

Classes began in September, about the same time Isabel (named for Isabel Cowie) was born. As the Wolfe's first child, she would make her father's interest in "child nature" more than an academic one. In his initial university year, Wolfe taught at least two, and possibly three, courses in philosophy. Enrollments were small: thirteen in his course on logic and eight in the one on ethics. His largest class, a course on scientific psychology, marked a new offering at the university, and enrolled fourteen students. In addition to the "General Psychology" course, in which he used George Trumbull Ladd's book *Elements of Physiological Psychology* (1887), Wolfe taught a class entitled "Experimental Psychology."

The experimental psychology class was a year-long course emphasizing the methods of physiological psychology and psychophysics that he had learned in Germany. The significance of this course is that it was accompanied by the establishment of a psychology laboratory, partly to support the course but also for Wolfe's own research. This laboratory was only the sixth to be founded in the United States, and it followed Wundt's founding of his laboratory by only a decade.[3] Wolfe's laboratory was perhaps unique at the time of its founding: it was probably the only psychology laboratory devoted exclusively to undergraduate education, a situation that would later lead to some controversy for Wolfe. Several senior students in the experimental course were allowed to pursue original research for college credit.

In addition to the teaching and laboratory instruction, Wolfe worked on his own research during his initial year at the university. In the year before his departure for San Luis Obispo, he had collected data from Nebraska schoolchildren regarding their ability to name colors, a study of the development of color

Wolfe's first psychology laboratory was established in 1889 in University Hall. (Photo courtesy of the Nebraska Historical Society)

vocabulary. He published the results of this research in a thirty-page monograph in the initial volume of the university's *University Studies* in the summer of 1890.[4] It marked his initial venture into child study, and its methodology, relying on thousands of observations of children across a wide range of ages, proved to be the strategy Wolfe would use for most of his later research. While writing this monograph, he also began collecting data for his second study of child nature. These studies, and others, are described in the next chapter.

At the conclusion of the academic year, Wolfe summarized

the activities of his department in a five-page report to Bessey.[5] His library fund of $217.50 had been used to add several recent works in ethics and logic, but most of the book purchases represented the new psychology: Wundt, Ebbinghaus, Stumpf, Fechner, and others. Wolfe had also increased the journal subscriptions from three to fourteen, including the donation of several of his own subscriptions. One of these was his collection of Wundt's *Philosophische Studien,* the journal in which Wolfe's dissertation had appeared.

The psychology laboratory consisted mostly of what Wolfe called "illustrative apparatus." Some of it he had brought with him from his study in Germany. The rest had been borrowed from his university colleagues in the natural sciences. The inventory included the following:

set of Marshall's physiological charts
Azoux's models of the brain, eye, and ear
stop clock
metronome
Hipp chronoscope
pendulum regulator for the chronoscope
Oliver's color-sense test
Helmholtz standard color sheets
"Drop apparatus (intensity of sound)"
"Revolving apparatus (memory for color)"
cards for illustrating color phenomena
drawings showing development of the nervous
    system and sense organs[6]

Although the collection was a meager one, it represented a good beginning for the laboratory, especially when one considers that Wolfe, unlike his University of Nebraska counterparts in the other sciences, received no equipment fund in his annual budget. Despite its small size, the collection is typical of the nature of laboratory work in the new psychology. As in the Leipzig laboratory, emphasis was on sensory functioning, particularly vision.

The principal instruments in an early psychology laboratory were devices for presenting stimulus events and recording devices for measuring the responses to those events. Examples of both exist in the inventory from the Nebraska lab. The drop apparatus was probably an acoumeter, a device that produces sounds of differing intensity by dropping a metal ball from different heights onto a glass plate. In the tradition of psychophysics, this apparatus was used in studies measuring intensity thresholds in sound, specifically the least perceptible sound intensity.[7] Measuring the speed of mental states meant recording response times. Wolfe's stop clock measured time intervals in quarter-seconds, and the chronoscope, manufactured by Hipp in Switzerland and serving as the workhorse of the early labs, was capable of measuring time in thousandths of a second.

Missing from the list is equipment used to measure senses other than sight or hearing, namely the chemical senses of smell and taste and the sense of touch. Common auditory items like tuning forks and other tone-generating devices were also absent, which is somewhat surprising given Wolfe's dissertation work on tone perception. Also absent are recording devices like the kymograph, whose rotating drum produced a paper record of response changes, typically magnitude, over time.

In addition to the library fund, Wolfe was given a departmental operating budget of one hundred dollars. The fact that he had no equipment fund is not surprising, although its absence frustrated him. The notion of an experimental laboratory within the traditional discipline of philosophy was still new enough to create suspicions about the validity of mental measurement. As a biological scientist, Bessey must surely have harbored reservations about this new psychological science, even though he apparently had very high regard for his new lecturer in philosophy. Pressing Bessey on the need for equipment, Wolfe argued, "The work of this Dept. ought to be chiefly scientific, but lack of equipment has compelled me to make it largely literary." He noted that at other universities, such as Clark, Pennsylvania, Wisconsin, and Indiana, psychology as a science was grouped with "the other natural sciences."[8]

In this report to Bessey, Wolfe also initiated his request for a formalized program in pedagogical psychology. He called for an elective course in pedagogics for would-be teachers, a class that would be based on physiological psychology and psycho-physics and that would include "original investigations in child nature." He stressed the importance of the new psychology for teachers, stating that such a course was necessary because "trainers of the mind ought to know whatever is known about mind." Keeping in mind the pedagogical program, Wolfe suggested a year-long applied psychology course that would focus on teaching, law, medicine, and theology. He asked for an additional room for the laboratory work, and concluded his report with one final plea, "I hope the scientific nature of this dept. may be recognized in the next apportionment of funds."[9]

In June, a month after filing his annual departmental report with Bessey and the regents, Wolfe wrote two more letters to the regents. One of these restated his request for a course in pedagogics and provided a rationale for it. He asked for additional library funds to buy pedagogical books and for $325 to purchase and construct some apparatus, as well as to remodel a basement room for the psychological laboratory.[10]

The other letter requested an advancement in Wolfe's faculty rank and, implicitly, an increase in salary. He wrote:

> Since your meeting in June 1889, several very respectable positions have been offered me, at considerable advance over my present salary, viz: Berkeley Cal. $2100.00, Los Angeles $1500.00 first year, $2000.00 afterwards. Two other offers at $1500.00 in small towns followed these. I may add that a friend connected with the Portland Or. schools assured me I could have their vacant principalship on application, salary $2000.00.

> Circumstances *compel* me to consider the present as well as the future. These offers came unsolicited and others may possibly follow. I would, therefore, respectfully ask your intention concerning the establishment of the *full professorship* of Psychology & Pedagogy, or Philosophy.[11]

The elective course in pedagogy was approved by the faculty, Bessey, and the board of regents, and the library fund for the philosophy department was increased for the 1890–91 academic year, largely for books to support the new course. And Wolfe was given an empty room in the basement of University

Hall, which he used as part of the laboratory, although he apparently did not receive the requested funds for the renovation. Further, the appeals for an equipment fund fell on deaf ears. There were more immediate needs in the university, particularly increased funding in the College of Agriculture to handle the growing student load there. Whether there was any adjustment to Wolfe's salary is not known; however, he was promoted to Associate Professor of Philosophy.

Wolfe's classes for his second year followed the pattern of the first, although enrollments had increased slightly. He began the course on pedagogical psychology, offered mostly to seniors bound for teaching careers. He also added an evening course, "Elementary Psychology," which was taught at the request of local teachers and former students, twelve of whom enrolled in the class. Much of his eight-page annual report to the board of regents this next year dealt with the nature of laboratory work in psychology and the need for additional funding of his department. In support of his request, Wolfe offered a description of the laboratory work for the year.

Laboratory work may be roughly grouped as follows; (1) Measurement of simplest mental phenomena, as the Least Observable Difference in sensations. (2) Determination of the relation between stimulus and sensation. (3) Testing Weber's Law. (4) Determination of the area or extent of consciousness for simple ideas. (5) Sense of time. (6) Time occupied by simple mental processes.[12]

Equipment was added to the lab during the year by using eighty dollars from the library fund for the department. Wolfe indicated in his report that he took that action after consulting with one of the regents. Most of the equipment added was built by the "university mechanic" and by Wolfe and his students.[13]

With added equipment, Wolfe indicated he could improve the instructional program for the psychology laboratory and promised the regents at least one monograph a year worthy of publication. Using an agricultural metaphor, he wrote, "No field of scientific research offers such excellent opportunities for original work; chiefly because the *soil is new.*"[14]

Wolfe wrote another letter to the board of regents in May

1891, perhaps the result of a request from Bessey or from a member of the board. This letter was an extended justification for the laboratory and included an attached budget for $1,818. It provided the details of the laboratory needs that were barely sketched in his annual report. In an effort to educate the board, Wolfe wrote:

The scientific nature of Psychology is not so generally recognized; hence I feel justified in calling attention to two points. 1st The advantages offered by experimental Psychology, as a discipline in scientific methods, are not inferior to those offered by other experimental sciences. The measurement of the Quality, Quantity and Time Relations of mental states is as inspiring and as good discipline as the determination of, say the percent of sugar in a beet or the variation of an electric current. The *exact* determination of *mental processes* ought to be as good *mental* discipline as the exact determination of processes taking place in matter. 2nd The study of mind is the most universally *applied* of all sciences. Because we learn so much about it from everyday experience is the reason perhaps, that it only recently has become an "exact" science. Whatever is known of mind is especially valuable in professional life, and particularly so in that profession whose object is the *training* of mind. The science of teaching depends immediately upon the results of psychological investigation. The progressive teacher must know, not only these results and the "methods" based thereon, but also how to investigate for himself.[15]

Wolfe's reference to measuring beet sugar was not chosen at random. In the 1880s, Americans had imported one hundred million dollars' worth of sugar. To reduce such imports, the U.S. Department of Agriculture was charged with developing an American sugar source. The cane sugar industry of Louisiana, seriously damaged by the Civil War, was well recovered but could not meet the American demand. Because Europe was succeeding with beet sugar, the USDA set up several field stations to test varieties of sugar beets. One of those stations was in Schuyler, Nebraska, and was supported by chemists from the university. The sugar beets of Europe did not grow well in American soil, thus researchers sought to develop an American variety with a comparable sugar content. At the time that Wolfe was addressing the regents, this line of research was very much in the news. By 1891, varieties had been produced that matched the European beets in terms of sugar content and tonnage, but the hard labor involved in beet farming limited its popularity and success.[16]

Wolfe's letter to the regents included a list of twenty-nine items needed for the laboratory. The two most expensive items on the list were a "tone instrument," at two hundred dollars, otherwise unspecified, and a set of tuning forks and resonators for one hundred dollars. It is possible that the tone instrument was the device that Wolfe had used in his dissertation research, an instrument consisting of three hundred sound vibrators. The items on the list were meant to complete the basic laboratory: models of the larynx and tongue, an esthesiometer to measure tactile sensitivity, a kinesimeter to measure muscle tension, and a time-sense apparatus to measure estimation of time. Some of the items listed seem to have been modeled after the battery of tests used in the anthropometric laboratory founded by Sir Francis Galton (1822–1911) in 1884 in England—for example, a craniometer to record skull measurements and a dynamometer to measure strength of grip.[17]

In the summer before the beginning of the 1891–92 school year, Wolfe was promoted to full professor. However, despite the elaborate listing of equipment and the extra letter of justification to the regents, he received no equipment fund. Letters indicate he kept the laboratory functioning by building most of the necessary equipment himself, aided by other faculty members and students. The departments of biology and physics, in particular, were helpful in loaning equipment. From biology Wolfe got microscopes, thermometers, and embryological specimens; from physics he borrowed tuning forks, resonators, electric motors, magnets, and batteries. He bought some necessary items using his own money, and on more than one occasion he overspent his departmental budget.

With the university's enrollment growing rapidly, enrollment in Wolfe's courses increased at an even higher rate. By the fall of 1892 he had seventy students in his general psychology class and was having trouble finding a room large enough to hold the lectures. He divided the class into groups of thirty to thirty-five students each, for laboratory demonstrations in psychology. This teaching format required more time from Wolfe, more laboratory space, and more supplies, some of them consumable, for the demonstrations. To aid him, the university authorized funds for a student assistant for the philosophical laboratory. Wolfe hired Ellen Hart Bentley, a senior student, to assist him in teaching the psychology lab sections.

For the program of study in pedagogics, Wolfe added courses on sensation, the history of education, child study, methods of teaching, and applied ethics, as well as a special course entitled "Attention, Memory, and Will." This class dealt with "those parts of psychology" that were of "most practical importance to the teacher."[18] Enrollments in these courses were also high, reflecting the fact that approximately 50 percent of the university's graduates were taking teaching jobs following graduation, even though half of that number would not remain in teaching as a profession. The large number of graduates starting out as teachers was due to the plentiful availability of teaching positions, necessitated by the rapidly growing school-age population and by the fact that Nebraska had only one, poorly supported state normal school at the time (at Peru). When the university and the Peru Normal School could not supply the teachers needed in the 1880s and early 1890s, more than a half-dozen private normal schools were created in the state.

Wolfe did not neglect philosophy while building his programs in psychology and pedagogy. He continued to teach the courses in ethics and logic, as well as a course on the history of philosophy. Yet it is clear that these courses got the least of his time and his interest. As early as 1892, only a few years after the first course on pedagogy was offered, Wolfe asked about the possibility of an additional faculty member in his department to handle the growing demand for courses in that field. In April 1893, as his academic responsibilities, partly self-imposed, continued to increase, he wrote to the regents:

Though I am devoting seventy hours per week to students, including the immediate preparation of lessons and notes yet I shall gladly carry a few extra hours next year and if possible the year after if the Regents will recognize the importance of this work by doing what is possible this biennium and announcing their intention to establish the chair of Pedagogy as soon as the man and the means can be found.[19]

The university had a new chancellor by this time, James H. Canfield, a promoter of ties between the state's public schools and the university. As part of his program to reach out to the people of Nebraska, Canfield established campus summer programs for teachers. That and other efforts at teacher training at the university caused friction with the normal school at Peru. The university tried to avoid the controversy by saying that it would restrict its role to graduate training and would leave the undergraduate preparation to Peru.[20]

Financially, Canfield and the university were in an impossible situation: rapidly accelerating enrollments with no increases in support from the legislature. Economic depression was worldwide, the Panic of 1893 striking Nebraska as well. Many professors found themselves, like Wolfe, with greatly increased work loads. The depression did not slow enrollments; Wolfe's classes got still larger. Canfield was able to help some by giving him two assistants for the academic year beginning in 1894. One was an undergraduate, the other was Rufus C. Bentley, an 1894 graduate in philosophy and psychology who had worked with Wolfe in the lab as an undergraduate student. Rufus Bentley would work with Wolfe for two years before leaving to pursue his doctorate in psychology.

Although helpful, the student and postgraduate assistants were not enough to make Wolfe feel he was keeping his head above water. He lamented to Canfield and the regents in his annual report of 1894–95, "It is now impossible to carry the work in a manner at all creditable to the professor in charge." His frustration was increased by a letter he received from one of his former students who was working on his doctorate in psychology at Cornell University. The student wrote that Cornell's philosophy department had eight faculty, none of whom taught more than six hours per week. At this point, Wolfe was teaching twenty-seven hours of regularly scheduled classes per week and had taught thirty the previous semester.[21]

The 1894–95 annual report is without a doubt the most negative of Wolfe's reports. Showing his exasperation, Wolfe expressed some bitterness over the treatment of his program relative to other departments. He wrote: "After looking over papers, themes, etc. there is very little time left for preparing lectures. I can feel the difference between the quality of last year's work and that of this year in spite of the fact that all day Saturday and six-hours Sunday are regularly given to University work, and that I know more than I knew last year." He called for an analysis of growth trends within the university by department and for a similar analysis of library usage, arguing that library funds were allocated evenly across departments without regard to course enrollments in those departments or the amount of library work students were given. He wondered about the number of "shelves of unused books and rooms of little used material, apparatus, or relics."[22]

Wolfe's accusation of inequities was not new to his correspondence with the chancellor. However, it was especially pointed and prolonged in the 1894–95 report. Further, he pointed to inequities in teaching loads, noting that compared with some of his colleagues in terms of class hours and students taught, he had a load three to five times greater. He acknowledged the serious financial problems of the university and said he did not expect any faculty additions in pedagogy or philosophy. Finally, he expressed particular dismay that the laboratory had never been supported, noting that although the Nebraska lab was one of the earliest to be founded, it had now fallen behind others that had been established later but that already possessed better equipment and facilities.

One explanation for the unusual negativity of this report is the possibility of a broken promise from the university's administration. Apparently Wolfe had received some indication from Canfield, or someone else within the administration, that he would receive substantial equipment funds for the 1894–95 academic year. Visiting Katharine's relatives in Philadelphia in the summer of 1894, Wolfe had written to a former student, "I have about $1200.00 for new equipment."[23] However, Wolfe's 1894–95 annual report made no mention of the funds. Instead, the report noted Canfield's remarks that the economic times required that, for the time being, the university must content itself with being a "teaching university." Wolfe repeated his annual request for equipment funds, this time asking for seven hundred dollars, acknowledging that the coming year would probably be the most difficult, financially, in the history of the university. He closed by stating, "The lack of equipment this year has been largely made up by additional time and energy on the part of the professor, and . . . this cannot possibly be continued another year even by working all day Sundays."[24]

There is nothing in the available university records to indicate any promise of a psychology equipment fund of twelve hundred dollars or any other amount. Given the economic problems of the university, it seems extremely unlikely that any such grant would have been made at that time. It is possible that Wolfe left Lincoln at the beginning of the summer having been told that the money would be forthcoming, and that subsequent financial analyses of the university's situation forced the administration to cancel that plan before the beginning of the fall term. Such a sequence of events would surely have compounded Wolfe's frustrations about the laboratory.

For Wolfe, the laboratory work was essential to learning about psychology. Again and again his letters and articles emphasized this point. He recognized the extra teaching responsibilities that lab courses required, but he was willing to add those to his duties, believing so vehemently in the worth of the laboratory experience. However, others did not share his view; they argued that laboratory instruction in psychology should not be part of an undergraduate curriculum but was more appropriate for graduate work. Both Bessey and Canfield, who seemed to admire Wolfe as a teacher, gave no evidence of being convinced of the worth of laboratory training in psychology. Neither responded positively to Wolfe's continued requests for equipment funds and laboratory space, with the possible exception of the promised funds for 1894–95.

Unable to convince the local authorities, Wolfe made his arguments public in a new journal, *Psychological Review,* founded by James McK. Cattell and James Mark Baldwin (1861–1934). The article, "The New Psychology in Undergraduate Work," reiterated many of the arguments Wolfe had made to the regents, and it sought to answer the criticisms he had heard so often.

It ought to be unnecessary to describe the effect on the student of a laboratory course in psychology, and yet, like chemistry and physics and biology and zoology, this new science will have to fight for every inch of ground. . . .

A valid objection [to the psychology laboratory] is . . . the time required for this work. Better supervision is required than for laboratory work in either chemistry or physics. This demands personal attention from the instructor in psychology. I think this objection is unanswerable. If instructors in psychology are unwilling to do this kind of work, we must wait until another species of instructor can be evolved. . . .

Logic and metaphysics and the dictionary may be well taught without a laboratory; physiological and experimental psychology require some *things* to see and *feel*. . . .

The junior . . . comes to psychology with more or less information concerning isolated facts of several sciences. [In a] general course of physiological and experimental psychology with laboratory practice . . . the needed facts of the associated sciences will be brought together; their relations will become clear, and gradually there will grow up a rational appreciation of the interdependence of the forces of nature.[25]

Ferdinand Courtney French, a professor of psychology at Vassar College, took issue with Wolfe in print, arguing that the proper place of experimental psychology was in the graduate school. French believed that teaching laboratory principles and procedures was self-serving for the discipline and the professor and was not in the best interests of the student. In his view, laboratory work was for training specialists and thus was not consonant with the principles of a general education. Apparently, French did not oppose chemistry or physics labs for undergraduates, believing those sciences were well enough established that their methods had withstood the test of time. But psychology, as a new science, could not make that claim.[26]

In trying to build his laboratory, Wolfe had to counter those arguments in addition to the more fundamental objection to the validity of psychology as a science. That objection had a long history of proponents—for example, Auguste Comte (1798–1857), who believed that psychology could never be a science because its object of study, unlike that of the other sciences, was itself.[27] Administrative resistance to the development of psychological laboratories is understandable, particularly in the 1880s when Wolfe began his laboratory. Laboratories were expensive educational endeavors, and those in psychology were no exception. Psychologists founding other early labs faced some of the same problems. Yet the resistance weakened a bit with the impact of William James's *Principles of Psychology* (1890), the two-volume work that summarized the scientific psychology of the time and, more important, described the enormous potential of laboratory psychology. This book attracted many of the next generation of psychologists, drawn by James's promises for a science unlocking the mysteries of mental life. Doctoral programs in psychology, with their accompanying laboratories, flourished to meet the new demand; in the 1890s, twenty-seven new American labs emerged.

Wolfe and Cattell were part of the first generation of American psychologists, and like most of that group, they received their training in Germany. But by 1900 there were more than 100 American psychologists who had received their doctorates at home, and by 1921, only 36 of 377 members of the American Psychological Association possessed doctoral degrees from foreign universities.[28] Most of the better-equipped laboratories and graduate psychology programs were in the East, but several in the Midwest enjoyed similar support, notably the principal state universities of Wisconsin, Iowa, and Indiana. Yet Nebraska did not follow a similar course, despite its early entry into laboratory work. With growing pressures from a depressed farm economy, accelerating enrollments without concomitant funding from the legislature, and a call to play a greater role in supporting agriculture, the University of Nebraska put its money where it expected the best return. For laboratory support, that meant biology and chemistry.

The philosophy department's curriculum did get some re-

lief in 1895 when the university established a program in pedagogy, hiring George Washington Andrew Luckey to fill the
chair. Luckey, like Wolfe, was a midwesterner, born in Indiana
in 1855. He too had worked in public schools prior to earning
his doctorate at Columbia University. His arrival marked the
beginning of the graduate program in education at Nebraska.
He took over several of the courses Wolfe had initiated, and he
established others at the graduate level. Luckey's interest in
child nature and psychology led him to form a close friendship
with Wolfe, one that would continue throughout their time together at Nebraska.

With Luckey's arrival, Wolfe added a new course, "Seminar
for Experimental Psychology," to the psychology curriculum.
In essence, this upper-level course allowed Wolfe to get course
credit for the work he was already doing in directing original
research projects for his students. The seminar was restricted
to those students who had completed the year-long experimental course, and all were required to carry out studies of
their own design. Wolfe did not entirely divest himself of his
teaching in pedagogy, adding a graduate course in child study
in 1896. This course also required original research projects by
each of the students.[29] Wolfe supported these research projects and the operation of the laboratory with whatever means
he had. He regularly diverted some library funds to the laboratory, until the administration explicitly forbade that practice.
He also overspent his departmental budget.

George MacLean, a professor of English from the University
of Minnesota, replaced Canfield as chancellor in 1895. He was
even less supportive of the psychology laboratory and far less
tolerant of Wolfe's budget deficits. In early 1897, when the deficit seemed too large to bear, MacLean asked Wolfe to provide a
list of the extra expenditures—totaling $75.86—and a ratio-
nale for such a deficit. In the letter sent to the chancellor and
the regents, Wolfe wrote:

> I do not consider these expenses as a "deficit" even in
> the technical use of the term. I am personally responsible
> for them and if the University doesn't wish to buy the
> articles from me when it is able to do so I shall preserve
> the remains as "heirlooms" in my family treasure house.

. . . As long as I work thirty five hours (35) per week
with my students I shall provide any needed inexpensive
article for my work without reference to the condition of
my departmental fund.[30]

Wolfe listed fourteen items, a dozen of which were less than
three dollars each; the most expensive item was a storage battery that cost nearly forty dollars. Several of the items were
purchased explicitly for the student projects. Apparently
Wolfe had bought these items with his own money once his departmental fund had been exhausted. However, he then submitted the bills to the university with a request for reimburse-
ment. Whether he was reimbursed is not known. What is clear
is that MacLean expected his department heads to remain
within their budgets. Wolfe's attitude of not considering his
overspending to be a deficit, "even in the technical use of the
term," must have grated on the new chancellor. It was one of
several disagreements that would lead to a serious clash between Wolfe and MacLean.

Although Wolfe fared poorly with the university's administration, at least in his repeated requests for support of his laboratory, he was exceptionally popular with students. His
courses were filled to overflowing, despite his reputation for
demanding a great deal of work. Students were "willing to
venture the work for the sake of the zest," according to one former student.[31]

Wolfe's lectures were extremely well received, partly because of his wit and his skill in illustrating his points with
memorable examples. The lectures were written in longhand,
averaging thirty pages for a typical one-hour address. Each
was titled and each ended with an announcement of the title of
the next lecture. The lectures were filled with examples from
the "practical world." His broad education and diverse interests showed in his classes; references were commonly made to
ancient history, art, literature, and the sciences.[32]

Discussion was welcome in Wolfe's classes, and he frequently interrupted his lecturing to direct a question at a particular student. His style was to provoke students to think, often playing the devil's advocate to interject positions that had
not been raised in discussions. He used humor and sarcasm,

Wolfe as a faculty member at the University of Nebraska (ca. 1890)

sometimes exploding "bombs" under his students to force them to react to his lecture or to what they had been reading. Yet he was not doctrinaire; students were praised for their reasoned arguments, regardless of whether their conclusions matched his own. He encouraged students to debate him, arguing that as passive vessels they would learn little.

Wolfe greatly enjoyed his dialogues with students and was known as a teacher who welcomed conversation with students. Adjacent to Wolfe's office was a reading room where reference books and journals were kept for his classes. Mostly, these were materials that belonged to Wolfe, but he made them available to students. Usually he sat in that reading room so that students could talk with him, and many took advantage of the opportunity.

Wolfe's lecture classes actually occupied little of his teaching time. In fact, he viewed such activity as the least important part of what he did as a teacher. Instead, most of his contact hours were spent in the laboratory, supervising the research of students, sometimes singly, often in small groups. These teaching hours were ones he added to his own duties; they were not required as part of his teaching contract. In addition he spent a considerable amount of time helping the students involved in independent research.

This involvement of students in research was of paramount importance in Wolfe's educational philosophy. In a lecture entitled "The Psychology of Research," he wrote: "Research is a mental groping by starlight towards the daylight of clearer vision. It begins in the slow, laborious *search* for facts in a narrow field. As material accumulates, relations appear. The mass ferments, and finally organizes itself into the semblance of a new, living idea."[33]

In Wolfe's opinion, research was the most important tool available to the teacher, and part of his plan was to use research to stimulate "mental growth" in his students once they left the university. His faith in research came from his analysis of the origins of individual knowledge. He wrote: "If we go back to childhood it is plain that research is the sole method of growth. Watch the child in his cradle investigating his fingers, his toes, his toys, the wall paper, anything that attracts his interest. Try the lecture method with him and observe his disgust! No, worse, his *indifference*. The beginning of interest and of development is in self-initiated movements."[34]

For Wolfe, a college education was not a vaccination that lasted for a lifetime or even several years. "The growing mind should be reinoculated with the virus of independent research for facts and new relations every week."[35] Mental ability was viewed as a product of wrestling with complex problems, of questioning rather than blindly accepting, of initiating exploration. This kind of activity, which he referred to as "original research," was lost as the child began to submit too fully to authority. It was the job of the university to restore that primitive and all-important process. Wolfe's belief in that premise is evidenced in his own life and in the way he taught his students. He promoted this position with his students in an effort to help them understand the rationale for the demands he made on them. Apparently he was quite successful because many did indeed "venture the work for the sake of the zest."

Some excellent students were attracted to Wolfe's courses, particularly students interested in science. One of the earliest was Walter Bowers Pillsbury, who graduated in 1892. Another was Madison Bentley, an 1895 graduate and brother of Rufus Bentley. Both of these undergraduates would earn doctorates in psychology from Cornell University, would head leading psychology laboratories, and would be elected to the presidency of the American Psychological Association. They are but two of an inordinately large number of psychologists who received their initial interest in psychology from Wolfe, a fact that would be documented by Fernberger's surveys of American psychologists in the 1920s.[36]

Wolfe infected his students with an appreciation of the importance of research and involved them intimately in that process of discovery. Further, he inspired them to pursue careers in psychology because of his belief in the ultimate promise of the field. Like Cattell and other psychologists of his generation, Wolfe believed psychology was *the* science of the twentieth century, and he gave that message to students repeatedly. "*It is the general belief* of physicists that we are on the eve of important discoveries in Physics second only to the discovery of the Copernican law of the solar system and of the law of gravitation. *Some psychologists* think the physicists will have to hasten if they are to claim the chief *attention of the* new century."[37]

It is important to understand Wolfe's educational philosophy to appreciate how frustrated he was by his inability to establish the psychology laboratory as he envisioned it. His conscientiousness as a teacher made it difficult for him to accept any situation that he viewed as less than ideal. It was hard for him to understand how his requests could be denied when what he was requesting was for his students and not for himself. The laboratory was needed not only to provide instruction but also to give Nebraska a position of leadership in this important new science.

Wolfe was as demanding of the university's administration as he was of his students. His students had a job to do, he had a

job to do in instructing his students, and the administration
had a job to do in supporting him and his students. How could
he and the students do their jobs if the administration failed to
perform its function? His passion for the profession of teaching and for the discipline of psychology would likely have
made him blind to the self-serving nature of that question.

In November 1895, Wolfe moved his psychology laboratory
from the always-under-repair University Hall to the newly
opened Library Hall, a building long delayed in its completion
because of a lack of funds. His quarters were new, but the
space given him was no larger than his old laboratory and apparently no better suited to his needs.[38] By this time, Wolfe
seemed reconciled to the fact that a comprehensive and well-
supported psychology laboratory was not a possibility, at least
not in the near future. Perhaps that was because of his recognition of the economic conditions in Nebraska, or an awareness
of his rather poor relationship with Chancellor MacLean.
Whatever the reasons, he ceased to ask, in print at least, for an
equipment fund for the laboratory.

There is another possibility for this change in Wolfe, and
that was his growing involvement in child study. Although his
pedagogical interests predated his arrival at the university, the
addition of Luckey to the faculty in 1895 provided Wolfe with a
colleague who had similar research interests. For Wolfe, research in psychology had meant the physiological and psychophysical work of the Leipzig lab, work that often required substantial instrumentation. However, in 1891 at an important
organizational session of the annual meeting of the National
Education Association, G. Stanley Hall, one of America's most
prominent psychologists, formalized what was to become
known as the child study movement.[39] Hall advocated that the
scientific study of children be based largely on the use of questionnaires.

Most of Wolfe's research to date had involved child study;
however, he had not been using survey methods. Here was a
way to teach the methods of science to his students, enhance
their intellectual development through hands-on research,
and involve them and himself in the discovery of practical information of great value to the training of teachers and parents

and to the education of students. And, as paper-and-pencil research, it could be accomplished with a minimum of expense. Wolfe did not stop teaching the lessons of Wundt's laboratory to his students. Those exercises were maintained as the research backbone of the experimental psychology course. Yet the child study surveys became an important research format for those students doing original research; the surveys dominated the graduate course in child study and were frequently used as well in the experimental psychology seminar.

Wolfe, referring to his research as "scientific pedagogy," became the chief proponent for child study within the university and throughout Nebraska.[40] He sought to use the methods of scientific psychology to discover all there was to know about the child: sensory capabilities, physical characteristics, humor, play, religious ideas, memory, attention span, and so forth. With this new knowledge, education would no longer be guesswork but would be a science. In short, child study united his two passions—education and psychology—while offering a way for a science of mental states to coexist with a science of sugar beets.

Chapter Four

Scientific
Pedagogy

A new round in the centuries-old debate on human nature, particularly the nature of the child, occurred in the later decades of the eighteenth century. One of the most influential participants was Jean Jacques Rousseau (1712–78), whose publication of *Julie, ou la nouvelle Héloïse* and *Émile* offered his views on the nature and education of children. The child was basically good; the purpose of education was to use reason to develop nature. Further, education should take place in the country, largely through direct interaction with the objects of nature. (An emphasis on the benefits of rural life for children is a theme that runs throughout the history of education.) In a one-on-one relationship, the teacher, by staying alert to the child's individual talents and needs, could present the child with new objects and new information. The child would never be forced to learn anything, not even reading or writing; rather, education was to be self-directed.[1]

Among those influenced by Rousseau was Johann Heinrich Pestalozzi (1746–1827). Like Rousseau, Pestalozzi rejected rote learning as an educational method. He placed great emphasis on children's emotional development, which he believed was largely determined by the relationship between teacher and learner. Pestalozzi was especially interested in educating the poor, arguing that the poor needed to learn a trade but also the rudiments of reading and writing. And this learning was to be self-generated, primarily through direct observation. His demonstration schools attracted many educators who came to study his methods, among them Friedrich Froebel and Johann Friedrich Herbart.[2]

Froebel (1782–1852), convinced of the importance of early experiences for the proper development of children, established schools where children could learn about nature from direct experience. Like Rousseau and Pestalozzi, Froebel believed that children were basically good and needed to be nurtured and cared for at an early age. Children were like young plants in that their own nature would allow them to develop properly, hence the name *kindergarten* for these schools. Froebel's kindergartens combined work and play. The work, where Froebel was involved, was gardening. Froebel felt gardening taught the child about nature through direct observation; it also taught the child about responsibility and cooperation because each child's plot was part of a larger garden. The main emphasis, however, was play, but carefully directed play.[3]

Herbart (1776–1841) did not subscribe to the idea of inherent goodness in the child. Instead, he viewed children as essentially neutral; the purpose of education was to instill moral values. Herbart was deeply interested in psychology and strongly believed that theories of education should be based on psychology, in particular on an empirical psychology. As an associationist, Herbart's views on the apperceptive mass (the mass of thoughts and ideas already in the mind) and his description of the five steps taken in acquiring new knowledge (preparation, presentation, association, generalization, and application) were very influential in educational circles of the nineteenth century. It was his emphasis on psychology as science, however, that would support the beginnings of the child study movement 60 years later. The publication of *Psychology as a Science* in 1824–25 marked his principal statement on the subject. In Herbart's view, psychology was an empirical science, based on direct observation, and was mathematical, but it was not experimental. His views on empiricism later influenced the child study movement via Fechner and Wundt, but his rejection of experiment led to a rift between those in the child study movement and American Herbartians.[4]

At the beginning of the nineteenth century, education was still largely the province of the middle class or the wealthy; universal education was not the norm. However, as the century progressed, systems of education in Europe and the United States began to diverge. The class system of Europe led to the establishment of a dual system of education, with separate schools for upper and lower classes. In the United States a system developed in which, at least in theory, every level of education would be available to those with the intellectual ability to take advantage of it. The poor would be educated for free. Following the idea of making education freely available (dependent on ability) came the idea of *requiring* that all people take advantage of the free education. Massive immigration, especially from Europe, gave the schools a new role, that of teaching the American culture to the new arrivals. Many of the new arrivals had little inclination for this indoctrination and had to be forced to attend. Massachusetts began compulsory attendance in 1852, and by the end of the century most states had followed suit. Nebraska's Populist legislature passed such a law in 1891, ending a twenty-year battle in the state over compulsory attendance.[5]

Although one of the purposes of the compulsory attendance laws was to change the immigrants, the immigrants were also changing the schools. The ideas of Pestalozzi, Froebel, and Herbart had their influence partly through Americans, like Wolfe, who had been exposed to these ideas in their study in Europe. But an equally important force for change was the immigrants, particularly German immigrants who established Froebel's kindergarten system in the United States. In the late 1800s, German immigrants made up a sizable portion of Nebraska's population.

Concurrent with changes in educational philosophy were changing attitudes toward children. Paralleling the rise of industrialization and urbanization in the nineteenth century were child-welfare reforms that reflected this change. Orphanages or foster homes provided care for otherwise normal children not receiving adequate care from their families. And special institutions were established for retarded children and for deaf, blind, or otherwise physically handicapped children. The passage of child-labor laws got children out of the factories; the passage of compulsory attendance laws got them into the schools.

The psychology of the late nineteenth century was strongly influenced by the work of Charles Darwin (1809–82) and Francis Galton. The former provided evidence for variability within species and for the importance of variation; the latter sought to measure variability, that is, individual differences, in humans. While Galton was testing people in his anthropometric laboratory in London, Wundt was measuring mental abilities in his subjects at Leipzig.

In the latter part of the nineteenth century, these forces combined to push for the *scientific* study of children. Immigration and industrialization heightened the need for schooling; the increasing enrollment of students sparked a demand from parents and teachers for information about how to teach children; psychologists interested in individual differences wanted to know how adult differences started; and the child-welfare workers wanted help in planning programs to help children. The child study movement attempted to meet these diverse needs. It was a movement that involved Wolfe for his entire professional life.

As noted in the previous chapter, the founding of the child study movement is credited to G. Stanley Hall. In 1882, Hall began a study of Boston schoolchildren, a study modeled after some similar surveys he had seen when he studied in Germany. The results of Hall's investigations were published as "The Contents of Children's Minds" in an 1883 issue of the *Princeton Review*. That paper is usually acknowledged to be the formal beginning of the child study movement.[6]

Like the German studies, Hall's questionnaire sought to establish what city children knew upon entering school. His questions asked these Boston children about beehives, sunsets, brooks, crows, rainbows, and growing wheat. Not surprisingly, he found much ignorance among the children tested. Hall's questionnaire favored children from a rural existence because of his belief that "knowledge of country life constituted 'general' knowledge and that it formed a superior mental training to knowledge of city life."[7] So convinced was he of the values of knowledge gained from country life that he urged city parents to take their children for visits in the country to improve their intelligence. Many parents and educators viewed Hall's questionnaire results as compelling evidence of the need for educational reform in America.[8]

Child study involved not only the mind but the body as well. Norms for schoolchildren were established, by age and sex, in physical dimensions, such as size of body and length of arms; in motor skills, such as strength of grip and running; and in perceptual capabilities, measured by tests of vision, audition, and smell. These studies were part of an emphasis on physical hygiene as it related to the development of mental abilities or as an indicator of the state of a child's mental development. Although these anthropometric studies were of lesser importance in the child study movement, they reinforced the belief in physical health as a condition for maximizing learning, and they stimulated additional studies to discover how school environments could be altered (e.g., ventilation, lighting, temperature) to enhance education.[9]

Hall certainly had strong feelings about the need for child study, largely in service to education, yet his founding of the *American Journal of Psychology* and his assumption of the presidency of newly established Clark University occupied much of his time in the latter half of the 1880s, allowing him a minimal role in child study. During this time the banner was taken up by the National Education Association (NEA), which began to hold sessions on pedagogy as a science at its annual meetings. However, child study as a movement had to await the reentry of Hall in 1891.

Hall attended the annual meeting of the NEA in Toronto in 1891, the first he had attended since 1885. He posted on a bulletin board a notice announcing a gathering of those interested in discussing child study; approximately 150 educators attended. The movement had its leader, and it was a role Hall was ready to assume. He believed that experimental psychology had reached a state of development that allowed the establishment of a true science of child study. In support of that belief he founded a new journal, *Pedagogical Seminary*, in 1891 to publish the results of scientific pedagogy. Hall dated the beginning of the child study movement from the 1891 meeting and not the 1883 article. The exact date of founding is of little importance; what is clear is that the movement had considerable momentum in the 1890s and enjoyed its greatest successes during that decade. It was bold in its hopes and in its promises, a boldness that attracted supporters and participants, as well as detractors.[10]

If the new psychology had any value as an applied science, surely it was in its application to education, a point stressed by Hall in his speeches and publications. A scientific study of child nature would provide the basis for improved teacher training, curricula, school facilities, and assessment of individual children and would thus build bridges between the universities and schoolteachers. Child study had other goals as well, for example, the improvement of parenting practices. In a lecture on child study, Wolfe wrote, "It is a shame that parents who have given years of their lives in acquiring general culture including History, Literature, Language, Science, and Music, should be left to learn the simplest facts of child nurture from their own experience."[11]

For Wolfe, and for most psychologists who were involved in child study, education was the focus of the work. As a teacher, Wolfe was disillusioned by the lack of knowledge about the learning process in children. His work was intended to investigate child nature in the service of teacher training. Beliefs of the rational approach to education, as opposed to an empirical approach, were that teaching was an art and that knowledge of child nature and skill in teaching were acquired in only one way—by teaching. Those in child study opposed that belief, arguing that such a practice was bad for children and teachers alike. Wolfe explained the problems of the rational approach:

It is however a common opinion that we learn human nature by chance contact with our fellows. My idea of human nature surely does not coincide with that intended by such advocates. Suppose however we grant the point that ordinary experience furnishes this knowledge. We cannot afford to wait a life time for guiding principles if they can be acquired earlier. As if a teacher were to say I can learn child nature and the way to educate, in the school room—by teaching—It is said that this course is well enough for the teacher, but it is rough on the children. I can't agree even with the first admission. *It is very seldom* endurable for the teacher. No teacher can afford to wait twenty five years for a professional reputation if it is possible to obtain as good a one in five years. The community cannot afford to give this much time, money, and *material* to make a teacher. We must know the common elements and the laws of development of child nature before beginning to teach.[12]

Clark University became the national center for child study, under Hall's leadership. Yet other universities, notably Illinois, Nebraska, and Stanford, established significant programs of their own. The focus of the child study work at Clark was the questionnaire. Although Hall did not originate the technique, his extensive use of questionnaires has caused the method to be associated with his name. The first of the Clark University child study questionnaires was on anger; it was printed in October 1894. Later ones dealt with such topics as crying and laughing, appetite and foods, obedience, perception of rhythm, interest in flowers, shame, imagination, dreams, aesthetic interest, and ambition. By 1903, 96 questionnaire studies had been completed, and by 1915 the number had swelled to 194.[13] The results of these surveys were usually published in one of Hall's journals, and copies of the questionnaires and results were available to educators all over the country through a child study clearinghouse organized at Clark.

In 1892, Hall began a series of summer programs at Clark, intended mostly for schoolteachers but attended as well by normal school faculty and administrators. These sessions generally lasted for two weeks, with classes scheduled from eight in the morning until ten at night. For several years, Rufus Bentley, Wolfe's former laboratory assistant, was in charge of these summer programs for teachers. The intensive study focused on the new psychology and the latest educational theory. Those attending these sessions were often involved in the collection of data for one or more of the Clark questionnaires. Indeed, Clark University became an archive for child study data. Teachers around the country collected questionnaire results, which were then forwarded to Clark to become part of a larger survey research program. Wolfe began a similar summer program for teachers at the University of Nebraska in 1894.

The Midwest seemed to be especially receptive to the child study movement. An impetus to that was a speech, almost a plea, that Hall gave in Chicago in 1893 as part of the World's Columbian Exposition. In it he urged states to establish child study societies. The first to be organized was in Illinois, founded at Champaign in 1894. Iowa established its society in late 1894, and Nebraska, with Wolfe and Luckey playing key roles through the Nebraska State Teachers Association, founded its society in December 1895. Kansas and Minnesota followed suit in 1896, and by 1910, another twenty states had officially established such groups. Most were in the West and Midwest, where educational traditions were not as firmly entrenched as in the East. Journals were established to publish the large volume of research, principally questionnaire studies, that was being generated. One of the earliest journals, preceding Hall's *Pedagogical Seminary* by a year, was the *North Western Journal of Education*, which began publication in Lincoln in 1890. Intended as an extension service of the university, the journal offered continuing education to Nebraska's schoolteachers and covered all fields, for example, literature, geography, and history. Wolfe wrote his first article for the journal in 1892, and in October 1894 he began writing a rather lengthy column, entitled "The Study of Children," which appeared in almost every issue through the early part of 1898.

Wolfe's role in child study in Nebraska cannot be overstated. His research on children, begun in 1886 while working with Nebraska schoolchildren, was published in 1890 and marked the initial publication on child study in the state. In that research, Wolfe tested approximately twenty-one hundred children, ranging in age from five to seventeen. He investigated age and sex differences with respect to tasks of color vocabulary, color discrimination, and color memory. The intent of the research was to discover children's abilities in these

Special child study issue of the *North Western Journal of Education* in 1896

areas "with a view toward stimulating the study of color in the schools."[14]

The study even included an investigation of seventy-four children diagnosed as color-deficient, perhaps the first study to look at color naming by color-weak and color-blind subjects.

Although this study did not use the questionnaire method, it was characteristic of the sensory studies of the child study movement and ranks as one of the earliest of such studies in American psychology.

This research had a substantial influence in shaping Wolfe's commitment to child study. Ten years after doing the research, he wrote:

> The effects of the work on the investigator more than justified the time. It created an interest in child study and gave an insight into child nature such as only long continued association with many children in the pursuit of a specific object could give. Whatever success has attended the attempts to teach psychology in the University of Nebraska is due more immediately to that first systematic work with children than to the three years training in German universities.[15]

It was a strong statement, to be sure, yet one that he believed in both heart and head.

Records indicate that Wolfe also gave the first public presentation in Nebraska on child study, a lecture before the Nebraska State Teachers Association in December 1892.[16] In this address, entitled "The Philosophy of Method," Wolfe called for teachers to study child nature to enhance their competence as teachers. He encouraged them to join with psychologists as original investigators, suggesting that they begin by practicing their methods as self-investigation. Partly, this practice was to provide them with training in introspection such as Wolfe had received in Leipzig. He urged:

> Procure a dozen bullets. Have a friend drop from three to twelve rapidly and evenly upon a piece of wood or met al . . . so that each bullet makes but one clear sound, then falls upon a soft cloth. . . . Make fifty trials per day for a week. Record each time the number dropped, and your guess. Observe regularity or irregularity of the decrease of correctness with increase of number, the limit of absolute certainty, and the effect of practice.

> Request your friend to hold in a closed hand a number of bullets. With your eyes on the hand, let him open and close it as soon as possible. Guess the number of bullets.

Tabulate answers, and note same points as above. Compare final results of eye and ear judgments obtained in this manner.

A little ingenuity will devise many other experiments of a similar nature. In carrying them on and in studying their results one cannot avoid introspection.

These simple experiments are well worth a few hours' time, not because one's personal peculiarity is important, but because the experience is sure to suggest a difference between things as they are and things as they seem.[17]

Teachers who showed a "germ of introspective talent" were encouraged to pursue that talent in the investigation of child nature. "The study of child nature [is] the foundation of pedagogy."[18]

The recruitment of teachers and parents as original investigators in child study was one of the hallmarks of the movement. Hall encouraged it wherever he went, including in his speech to the 1893 annual meeting of the Nebraska State Teachers Association. Teachers and parents had ready access to children for hours each day; using these two groups to collect data on child nature was the only practical way to deal with the immensity of the task. The state societies played a role in organizing teacher and parent groups to participate in specified research projects.

The use of lay investigators produced one of the principal objections to the child study movement. Among the critics were some prominent educators and psychologists, for example, William James and James Mark Baldwin. Baldwin had initially been a supporter of and contributor to the movement but later condemned it as a "fad." He argued that teachers conducting child study research were being deceived in "thinking that they [were] making contributions to science."[19]

The harshest of the critics from psychology was Hugo Münsterberg (1863–1916), the director of the psychology laboratory at Harvard University. Writing in an 1898 issue of *Atlantic Monthly,* he warned teachers:

This rush toward experimental psychology is an absurdity. Our laboratory work cannot teach you anything which is of direct use to you in your work as teachers; and if you are not good teachers, it may even do you harm, as it may inhibit your normal teacher's instincts. . . . You may collect thousands of experimental tests with the chrono-scope and kymograph, but you will not find anything in our laboratories which you could translate directly into a pedagogical prescription.[20]

Münsterberg's chief objection to child study was the use of teachers and parents as data collectors. He wrote, "The work must be done by trained specialists or not at all." He also opposed child study on the grounds that it depersonalized the child and would alter the way teachers related to children. He feared that an analysis of the individual abilities of children would eventually dissolve their personalities into elements. And, he said, "Love and tact have nothing to do with a bundle of elements."[21] Finally, Münsterberg was critical of the lack of theory guiding child study research, noting, "Child study . . . has for its aim only the collection of curiosities about the child, as an end in itself." In his view, the value of child study for psychology was akin to the value of hunting stories for scientific biology.[22]

In truth, Münsterberg's assessment of the child study data was partially correct. Certainly many of the "studies" were poorly conceived, administered, and interpreted by individuals with little or no training in the methods of science. And, with the exception of Hall's work, little of child study owed any of its existence to psychological or educational theory. However, Münsterberg's vehement denial of psychology's applicability to education was as unrealistic an assessment as the claim that psychology held the answers to all educational questions.

Not surprisingly, Münsterberg's denouncement of the child study movement produced a flurry of responses disputing his claims.[23] Hall responded with an article in *Forum* in 1900, asserting that child study was in itself an act of love of children because parents and teachers were motivated to gain the new knowledge that would better help them raise and teach these children. Hall criticized those parents who did not "love their children intelligently enough to study them."[24]

And by pointing to the use of lay observers in anthropology

and biology, Hall also reacted to the criticism that data collected by untrained observers would have little value. He noted that even Charles Darwin had relied on the observations of nonscientists. Further, he argued that the familiarity of parents and teachers with their children could lead them to make observations that might be missed or misinterpreted by a scientific observer not acquainted with the child.

Clearly Hall recognized the variance of quality in the scientific work in child study, work that he had described as ranging from "utter worthlessness to the very highest value." But he was dismayed that the critics of child study chose to focus their attacks on the poorest of the work, "vanquishing the weaklings," as he referred to it.[25]

Wolfe answered the critics as well. "The teacher more than any one else can easily make valuable contributions to the knowledge of child nature and its development. The most fertile field, today, for original research in *any* department of science is in the study of the child before his tenth year. In a few years this knowledge, so easily obtained will be common property of teachers but the opportunity for investigation will then be narrower."[26] A portion of Wolfe's summer programs at the university, and later at a junior normal school in O'Neill, Nebraska, emphasized methods in child study to be used by the teachers, administrators, and parents in attendance. Guest instructors from Illinois, Minnesota, and Ohio were brought in for these summer sessions.[27]

Wolfe began offering a child study course in the fall of 1892, enrolling "nine or ten students" who had completed the year-long course in experimental psychology.[28] When Luckey arrived in 1895, Wolfe began teaching a graduate-level child study course, requiring an original investigation from each of the students. His students studied such topics as children's interests in stories (nature stories, classic myths, fairy tales), poetic abilities, perceptions of symbols, preferences for pictures, development of number sense, imitation, and ideas about Santa Claus.[29] Many of the students' investigations were published in the *North Western Journal of Education,* often concluding with a section entitled "pedagogical value." The inclusion of the pedagogy section was not a reaction to the critics' charges that child study data had little practical value for the teacher. Some emphasis on the pedagogical relevance of the research had long been a part of Wolfe's articles. Every investigation he undertook, both published and unpublished, was applied, reflecting what he called the "appeal of the starving world."

In his lectures on child study, both to his classes and to the teacher and parent groups with whom he met frequently, Wolfe described the research methods of child study. For parents and teachers he emphasized naturalistic observation involving well-delineated categories of data collection. For example, he suggested the systematic recording of children's physical characteristics such as hair (dark/medium/light, wavy/straight/curly/"frizzly," thick/thin), eyes (gray/blue, deep set/projecting/far apart, round/narrow), and face (long/short, intelligent/dull, expression changing/constant). Children were to be observed at work and at play in terms of categories such as movements (fast/slow, restless/quiet) and temperament (strong/weak, quick/slow).[30]

Exactly what teachers and parents were to do with such data is not clear. The observations were not posed for any phrenological or physiognomic reasons, although some of the descriptors used in the categories clearly could be classified as such. Instead, Wolfe suggested the data could be used to supplement mental tests of the popular anthropometric variety espoused by Galton and Cattell. Teachers were encouraged to record their observations as part of a permanent file to be kept on each child. Thus subsequent teachers could draw on earlier observations, noting progress or lack of it. Physical variables were important in understanding children's progress in school. In describing children, Wolfe wrote: "Their physical condition is the most powerful factor in their development. The influence of body upon mind comes home to us more strongly as we observe the effects of health, exercise, ventilation, nutrition, and fatigue."[31]

The testing of aptitudes and abilities was the second child study method Wolfe recommended. In addition to sensory tests of sight, hearing, and touch, he suggested tests of memory, imagination, attention, reasoning, and moral ideas.

Knowledge from these tests would aid in classifying children, thereby allowing the needs of the individual child to be met. One of Wolfe's greatest hopes for the child study work was that it would lead to the development of a measure of intelligence. "If there be such a thing as *general intelligence* the index to it will be discovered. If all intelligence shall be shown to be special intelligences uninfluenced by each other, then we shall catalog them and will soon be able to slip the child into his appropriate filing case."[32]

Hall was not very enthusiastic about mental testing. However, as it became more successful, partly at the hands of his own students, he attempted to claim it as a part of child study. In contrast Wolfe, as early as 1890, espoused the belief that such testing was critical if teachers were to do their job. His research on abilities emphasized sensory capabilities in sight and hearing, focusing particularly on sensory deficits and the ways in which these affected learning. However, he also investigated some aspects of cognitive functioning, such as judgments of size and weight, and language skills. These studies usually involved psychophysical methods and rarely used questionnaire methods except as an adjunct.

Wolfe believed in the value of questionnaires as collections of facts that provided a strong basis for generalization, although he acknowledged they were not strictly scientific. Yet his students regularly used questionnaires in their original research projects in the advanced classes, and they did so with his encouragement. He was very willing to allow students to pursue topics of their own choosing, even if the subjects were of no interest to him. He believed his role as instructor was to guide students in the conceptualization, methods, and interpretation of research. Enthusiasm for the work would come from the inherent interests that students brought to the topics they chose to investigate.

Interestingly, Wolfe rarely used students to help him collect data for his own research. He was concerned that the conditions for the research be uniform with respect to a single experimenter, a principle that perhaps came from his exposure as a student to Ebbinghaus. Characteristic of Wolfe's psychophysical work was a study he began in 1893 to investigate the effects of size on judgments of weight. Data were collected over a period of four years in which subjects lifted paper bags, lead and wooden weights, and brass cylinders. The work "was suggested by the well-known difficulty of judging the weight of light bodies in terms of pounds, or of heavy bodies. A pound of lead was known to be psychologically heavier than a pound of feathers."[33]

In this investigation, Wolfe concluded that despite considerable experience with substances differing in specific gravity, individuals are not very accurate in weight estimation. He noted that perceptual errors increased as the differences between the specific gravities of two substances increased and that, even with practice, individuals were not likely to decrease the magnitude of their errors. Visual information dominated kinesthetic information with the result that large errors in weight estimation were made by the subjects.

The pedagogical intent of the research was made clear by Wolfe. "Whether the sense of sight is assuming the functions of the other senses to their detriment is, perhaps, uncertain. The relative importance of the senses is undoubtedly changing, and in this way sight is certainly distancing all others. Unless our power of acquiring knowledge is also increasing, it follows that the other senses must lose."[34] Wolfe wondered if sight was developing at a faster rate than were the other senses, thus thwarting full development in those senses—in this study, the muscular sense stimulated by lifting different weights. If that was found to be true, schools would need to structure activities to increase the proficiency of the other sensory systems. The results of Wolfe's dissertation on tone memory had convinced him of the possibility of improved performance by training the senses. Drawing from the legacy of the British empiricists, Wolfe argued that psychologists needed to understand the interaction of the senses and the limits of those senses if the process of learning was to be improved. His focus on sensory defects, mentioned earlier, reflected his view of improving learning in "problem" children by enhancing other senses in a compensatory fashion.[35]

Although Wolfe repeatedly wrote and spoke about a new pedagogy based on the research of the new psychology,[36] his chief role in child study was not as a researcher. Instead he emerged early as the dominant figure in promoting child study throughout Nebraska. He was disappointed that the state society was not begun in 1893, the year that Hall spoke to the annual meeting of the Nebraska State Teachers Association. Based on his own keynote address to the same body the year before and on a round-table session on child study, Wolfe felt the state was primed to organize such a group, either within the teachers' organization or as a separate entity. However, he wanted the impetus for the society to come from the schoolteachers; he was unwilling to propose such a society, feeling it would likely fail unless the idea was generated from the ranks of those who worked daily with children.[37]

At the meeting the following year there was another round table on child study led by Grace B. Sudborough, the principal of the training school in Omaha. This session drew more than half of the teachers in attendance, despite the fact that four other sessions were being conducted simultaneously. Sudborough was one of several administrators and teachers who called for a state child study society. A committee was formed to draft a constitution to present to the body at its 1895 meeting; Wolfe and Luckey served on that group. The constitution was approved, establishing the Nebraska Society for Child Study. Reflecting on the wait, Wolfe wrote: "A state organization could have been formed and 'carried' *two years before*. It will now walk alone, and with the assistance already assured may be able even to run a little."[38]

The executive committee of the society comprised the elected officers and several others dictated by positions outside of the society. Those included the professor of pedagogy at the University of Nebraska; the state superintendent of education; and the president of the normal college. Thus, as professor of pedagogy, Luckey held one of the seats. Wolfe was also elected to the initial executive committee in one of two at-large seats.

The constitution established local child study groups, designated as round tables. These were formed by petition to the society "whenever there are five or more persons in the same locality wishing to unite upon the study of children." An advisory board was also established in the constitution to assist the round tables in planning meetings and conducting research. One of the positions mandated for this board was the "professor of experimental psychology." The designation clearly referred to Wolfe, although his university title in 1895 was Professor of Philosophy.[39]

The stated purposes of the society, as well as its organizational structure, were modeled after those of the Illinois Society for Child Study.

1. To stimulate among the teachers and parents of this state a study of all the phases of child nature and child growth, in order better to adapt education to the individual needs and capacities of the child.

2. To facilitate the investigations of teachers and parents now in progress, by concentrating the observations and researches along certain definite lines in which all will be interested, and by establishing local and central offices in which the data from all parts of the state can be collected and collated.

3. To acquaint teachers and parents with the results already obtained from the study of children, and to show how this knowledge can be used to advantage in the treatment of children.[40]

The charter membership consisted of 128 people, representing fifty-one Nebraska cities. Lincoln had the largest representation with thirty-nine, Omaha was second with eleven. There was even a member from South Dakota and another from Wyoming. Wolfe and Luckey were the only members from the University of Nebraska.

In the years that followed the founding of the society, Wolfe spoke frequently at the meetings of the local round tables, at education meetings, to parent groups, and at commencement activities. He was a popular speaker, knowledgeable in the child study literature and inspiriting in his call for his audiences to join "the greatest educational movement" the world had ever experienced.[41]

Indeed, child study was part of sweeping educational reforms occurring in Europe and America at the turn of the twentieth century. In Nebraska, the emphasis was on teacher training, particularly for the rural schools, where many teachers had completed no more than six or eight years of formal schooling. The Nebraska Society for Child Study helped to organize local groups in the battles for educational reforms. Teacher certification had been a local matter, usually handled within the county, and many communities had no certification requirements at all. In 1897 the University of Nebraska was authorized to issue teaching certificates, which, after a three-year probationary period, were good for life. It was no system of quality assurance, but it was a beginning and was significant, in part, because it gave the university some official responsibility for the state's teachers.

At the beginning of the twentieth century, the debate in Nebraska concerned the need for additional normal schools and the establishment of a teachers college in the university. Luckey, then head of the Department of Education, opposed such a college, arguing that teacher preparation should be left to the normal schools, although he acknowledged a role for the university in extending the undergraduate preparation of teachers. He felt that could be accomplished through the university's summer programs, which had been well attended by schoolteachers and administrators. Child study courses were always a popular part of those summer sessions.

After legislative debates about the quality of teachers—making teachers of "those whom God Almighty never intended should be teachers"—a second normal college was founded at Kearney in 1903. Four years later the legislature enacted a teacher certification law that required teachers to graduate from a college, university, or normal school. And public and legislative pressure caused the university to expand its offerings in the education department, for example, adding a course in school management in 1906. Two years later Luckey's Department of Education became a separate college. It endured a difficult beginning when Luckey, perhaps because of his opposition to an undergraduate program in education at the university, was passed over for dean of the college. Instead, the position went to Charles E. Fordyce, an administrator at a local Methodist college, Nebraska Wesleyan University. As the need for qualified teachers increased beyond the capabilities of the Lincoln campus and other existing schools, two additional normal colleges were established by the legislature, one at Wayne in 1910 and another at Chadron in 1911.[42]

Of course some authorities opposed the changes in education. According to Münsterberg, the new school reforms were only making a bad situation worse. He argued that teachers were of low quality, undereducated, and poorly trained for teaching. And he doubted whether teachers could be trained, believing that teaching ability was based on natural instincts. Hall agreed that many teachers were poorly qualified; however, he lauded the changes that were remedying that situation. He called for teachers to be grounded in the knowledge of child nature as generated in child study but also to be better prepared in basic education, for classes to be smaller, for salaries to be higher, and for politicians to leave the teachers alone.[43]

Beyond educational reform, the child study movement also influenced other areas in the early 1900s. For example, an interest in children's activities outside the schools promoted the development of neighborhood playgrounds and the establishment of organizations, such as the Boy Scouts, for organized play and moral training.[44]

The child study movement was, in some respects, the "pop psychology" of its day, and scientific psychologists and the nonscientific public responded in much the same way they do today. Scientific psychologists mostly rejected it; the public embraced it with great enthusiasm. Yet the movement began to lose its popularity in the first decade of the twentieth century, partly because of the public's dissatisfaction with some of Hall's views. In his 1906 book *Youth: Its Education, Regimen, and Hygiene,* written as a textbook for normal-college students, Hall defended his views on a number of controversial topics, such as corporal punishment, tolerance for male misbehavior as natural and acceptable, separate educational curricula for women, opposition to coeducational high schools, the "unfortunate" predominance of women as schoolteachers, the belief that education was to be reserved for those who could intellectually profit from it, and a call for education to include moral and religious training.[45]

Hall's 1906 book was an abridged version of his two-volume

work on adolescence, published in 1904. That book was banned in many libraries because of its explicit discussions of adolescent sexuality. Dorothy Ross, a historian and biographer of Hall's, has said that the book was Hall's "crowning effort in child study, but it followed his far-ranging mind quite beyond the pedagogical purposes and mental limits of the movement."[46]

Shortly thereafter, Hall ceased to lecture on education or child study. He turned to interests in psychoanalysis, the psychology of aging, and the psychology of religion, and ultimately to the self-reflection of his two autobiographies. He continued to publish occasionally on child study, but by 1911 he had effectively abandoned the movement, a ship that he clearly recognized as sinking.

Changes marking the final days of the movement included the rise in prominence of other universities in training education faculty, notably the Teachers College of Columbia University; the alteration of the NEA's Child Study Department into the Department of Child Hygiene; the emergence of the mental testing movement, largely fostered in America by three of Hall's students, Henry Herbert Goddard (1866–1957), Lewis Terman (1877–1956), and Frederick Kuhlmann (1876–1941)[47]; the experimental methods for child research offered by Edward L. Thorndike (1874–1949) and John B. Watson (1878–1958); and, perhaps most important, the establishment of child research centers to use these new observational and experimental methods.[48]

With the establishment of these new centers, such as the Iowa Child Welfare Research Station founded in 1917, the child study movement gave way to the child development movement, whose research was largely centered in university laboratories. Thus child study "bridged the gap between pseudoscientific, philosophical speculations, and a true science of the child, between 'rational' education and educational psychology, between sentimental and scientific principles of child rearing."[49]

The child study movement was never successful in fulfilling its grandiose ambitions: psychologists searched for laws of human behavior in child study, university administrators sought a better means of training teachers, educators desired better quantitative measures of schools' performances, social workers wanted data that would provide a base for political advocacy, clinical psychologists wanted normative data on emotional and cognitive development, and parents needed information on child rearing.[50] Too many people from too many diverse perspectives with too many different needs made those ambitions impossible to realize. However, the child study movement was the first effort to study children scientifically and to apply psychology to the practical problems of those who dealt with children.

Wolfe never lost his faith in child study and stayed active in that work for the remainder of his career. True to his almost religious conversion to the field, his message to teachers and parents was consistent.

If you would know the child make an effort to study it in any way that interests you. Persist and you will soon have all the methods of the specialists. This field is the most remarkable in nature. No earnest work can be lost. As soon as you learn one thing two others present themselves for answers and you are led on and in, until you are compelled to study the literature of the subject for your own peace of mind. The simplest and most effective rule, then, is BEGIN. Do SOMETHING, it matters little what you do at first, you will find it leads straight into the midst of this new world. And if you would not be drawn in I warn you to shun even the appearance of Child Study.[51]

Chapter Five

Politics in
the Academy

The 1895 school year began on a more promising note for Wolfe. Although the university's failure to provide an equipment fund for the psychology laboratory in the previous year had not been forgotten, Wolfe now had a small amount of money for equipment. He wrote to Titchener at the beginning of the school term, indicating that he planned to buy one of the new chronoscopes and asking Titchener's advice on the best model.[1]

Wolfe seemed to have regained some of his optimism because prospects for the future held some promise. Already his work load had been helped by the arrival of George Luckey, who handled all of the pedagogy courses except one, leaving the psychology and philosophy offerings for Wolfe. What Luckey's presence meant was that Wolfe was free to devote more time to instruction in the psychology laboratory. And he desperately needed that time. For the fall 1895 term, Wolfe had eighty-five students in the beginning psychology class, with each of them participating in two laboratory hours per week. In addition there were twelve students in the experimental psychology class, which required four hours or more of laboratory work each week.[2]

In late September the philosophy department moved into its new quarters in Library Hall—not larger and not designed

Wolfe's psychology laboratory in Library Hall (ca. 1896)

for psychology, but new. The good news for Wolfe was that the administration had approved the addition of an instructor in philosophy for the next academic year, someone who could teach some of the philosophy courses and also help Wolfe in the enormously time-consuming work with students in their laboratory and research projects.

For that position, Wolfe thought of his former student, Walter Pillsbury, who was completing his doctoral work in psychology with E. B. Titchener at Cornell University. Wolfe wrote to Pillsbury in January and again in March 1896, alerting Pillsbury to the possibility of a faculty position at Nebraska yet indicating that he would not be able to make a firm offer until the regents met in April to vote on the position.[3]

Wolfe met with Chancellor MacLean in mid-April and learned that the chancellor was supporting his request for the instructor's position and that MacLean expected the board of regents to approve it at the meeting the following week. Wolfe considered this a true gain, "a mark of great significance for

Philosophy in the university," because the university's proposed budget for the coming year had no increase.[4]

Later that day, in a mood of guarded excitement, Wolfe wrote to Pillsbury:

> We can offer you $800 for the year Sept. 15th to June 15th. . . . You would have three hours per week in Logic, first semester, with (perhaps) two hours in Logic second semester, provided you can get students for an advanced course. At least twenty hours per week in laboratory through the year. And either a three hour course in hist. of Philos.—Introductory or, in case I decide to give that myself, you would have charge of the *laboratory* work of my second year class in Exp. Psy. During the second semester I would like to have you offer your course in Optics or any other one or two hour course (per week) that you have worked up.
>
> Your work would thus be *equivalent* to six hours of class work and twenty hours with students in the laboratory each week. You would have assistance in the laboratory work and I would do most of the planning for this work as it is merely to supplement my class work.[5]

Wolfe encouraged Pillsbury to accept the offer, yet he was quite frank about his perceptions of the situation at Nebraska. He wrote: "Regarding the future, nothing can be safely said. All is uncertain in Nebr." And he reminded Pillsbury of the suffocating work load of the department. "[There are] fair prospects for fruit, but it is not the fruit of scholarship, it is the fruit of practical influence." In what seems almost an aside, Wolfe informed Pillsbury, "If I should die or be expelled, you would be in direct line of succession."[6]

At the time of this letter, Wolfe already had an application from Edgar Lenderson Hinman, a recent doctoral graduate from Cornell whose interests and training were principally in philosophy, not in psychology. Wolfe commented to Pillsbury that he felt Hinman would not find the nature of the work at Nebraska to his liking.

With Titchener's encouragement, Pillsbury decided to remain at Cornell. He wrote to Wolfe at the end of April to decline Wolfe's offer. In his letter, Pillsbury expressed some uncertainty about his decision, and Wolfe responded by offering to restructure the job if there was another arrangement more suited to Pillsbury's liking.[7] Yet Pillsbury's decision stood; Wolfe expressed regret but clearly supported Pillsbury's judgment.

Hinman persisted in his quest for the job, writing to Wolfe that it was just the kind of position he wanted. And Titchener sent a short letter to Wolfe supporting Hinman for the job. Although favorably impressed by the letters Hinman had written, Wolfe remained uncertain about him. He wrote to Pillsbury:

Now what I need to know is not the things people are likely to write. . . . What is the value of his *personality*? What is he in the world for? Has he any energy or push? Will he help my department's *influence* over students? Can *students* get within talking distance of him and will they get any inspiration from him? . . . Do you think he could give the same simple experiment separately to 100 students and make it just as interesting to the 101st?[8]

Eventually Wolfe decided to take a chance with Hinman, who was hired as an instructor in philosophy to begin in the fall 1896 term.

The Department of Philosophy, which only two years previously had had separate programs in philosophy, psychology, and pedagogy, all taught by Wolfe, now had spun off a very successful program in pedagogy headed by Luckey and had added another faculty member to share in the responsibilities of the other two programs. Enrollments continued to be among the highest in the university, and Wolfe was among the most popular instructors. Graduates of the philosophy and pedagogy programs were quite successful in pursuing graduate work or taking positions as school principals and superintendents. From an outsider's perspective, the situation in the philosophy department appeared healthy. Yet trouble brewed within the university.

During the 1895–96 school year, MacLean criticized Wolfe for his teaching of evolution. Apparently MacLean did not object to the teaching of the theory; however, he charged that Wolfe placed too much emphasis on evolution's opposition to religion. On hearing MacLean's charge, seventy-nine students signed a statement sent to the chancellor.

> Having been informed that the religious influence of Dr. H. K. Wolfe is thought to be detrimental to the higher spiritual growth of students taking work in his department, we the undersigned, professed Christians, having taken work in his classes, deem it just to him to make the following statement.

> Dr. Wolfe in his class-room tries to present to his students all possible sides of a question, and then lets them choose for themselves. We believe that we have, in no way, been injured by his teachings, but on the contrary, have been inspired to a higher and nobler life by having come in contact with him.[9]

It is not known if this issue was raised again with Wolfe, nor if it was reported to the board of regents.

In April 1897, a few days before the regents were to meet in Lincoln, MacLean and Wolfe met to discuss Wolfe's requests for his departmental budget and his plans for the department for the 1897–98 academic year. About the meeting, Wolfe wrote: "The chancellor never seemed more interested and never appeared to be more confidential and friendly. The disposition of the fund allotted to my department was left entirely to my judgment, and my every suggestion regarding it was adopted."[10]

Wolfe was called to meet with the chancellor again, on April 28. He assumed the meeting was about the Department of Philosophy's budget for the coming year, and so he took with him notes that he had been preparing for his annual departmental report. The chancellor opened the meeting by telling Wolfe that the regents had decided that Wolfe's services would no longer be required after the close of the current school year.

There is no indication that the charges against Wolfe were discussed at this meeting. According to Wolfe's version of the meeting, the chancellor had one item of business after announcing Wolfe's dismissal, and that was to determine the manner in which the termination would take place. MacLean suggested three possibilities: resignation, leave of absence at half pay without any expectation of return, or discharge. Wolfe said he would not resign, nor would he voluntarily take a leave of absence. By Wolfe's own account, he was stunned by the news and had "not the least suspicion of such action."[11] MacLean gave the information to the press the following day, and reports of Wolfe's dismissal appeared in the newspapers on April 30.

Rumors that Wolfe had been dismissed began circulating on campus on the morning of April 29. Almost immediately, students began to distribute petitions supporting him. According to newspaper accounts, nearly one thousand of the university's approximately sixteen hundred students had signed the petitions by the close of the day.[12] Those students engaged in the petition drive urged the signers to attend chapel services the following day to express their disapproval of the regents' action. The student newspaper, the *Hesperian*, described the chapel service.

Even the casual observer who entered chapel yesterday morning could see something out of the ordinary had taken place—or was about to take place. Not a seat was unoccupied, many were standing. Cries of "Wolfe! Wolfe! Wolfe! what's the matter with Wolfe?" "He's all right," were followed by vigorous applause.

During this time the Chancellor and regents took seats on the platform. . . . When he [MacLean] stepped forward to lead the devotional exercises he incidentally remarked that it gratified him to see department students so loyal to their professor. He said Dr. Wolfe was "all right" *in many ways*. The remark was received with hisses from several parts of the chapel as if certain students thought the statement ironical.[13]

After the chapel services the student leaders called a mass student meeting to be held in the chapel a little before noon. Again the chapel was packed. Students drafted several resolutions, including one asking the regents to delay their decision on Wolfe until after their June meeting. Another resolution apologized to the chancellor for the hissing during the chapel services. A committee of students was appointed to meet with the regents. However, the meeting never took place because the regents left town immediately after the adjournment of their board meeting.

The local newspapers, including the *Hesperian,* carried Mac-Lean's version of Wolfe's firing.

> . . . the Chancellor said that members of the board of regents asked him if Dr. Wolfe were following the official advice given him by the executive committee of the regents a year ago through the Chancellor. This advice was that Prof. Wolfe should devote himself to his own department and not meddle with other departments. The Chancellor told the regents that Prof. Wolfe had not followed this official advice. The regents asked the Chancellor what policy he recommended. The Chancellor stated that he thought it for the best interests of the university that Dr. Wolfe's relations with the university cease. The work of Dr. Wolfe in his department was not attacked. Religious or political scruples did not enter into the question of demanding the resignation. It was held that Dr. Wolfe was disloyal in not cooperating with the rest of the faculty.[14]

The specific charges against Wolfe were never made public, nor is there any record that Wolfe ever received any written communication from the regents or MacLean describing the reasons for his dismissal. By rumor, and based on MacLean's public statement, the charges became "meddling in other departments," "failing to heed the regents's warning," and "noncooperation with the faculty."[15]

For the month of May the controversy largely disappeared from the newspapers. Wolfe stayed out of direct conflict, allowing some of his friends to see if the situation could be reversed. The regents would return to Lincoln in mid-June for commencement exercises and their regularly scheduled board meeting. It was hoped that they might be persuaded to reinstate Wolfe. In the beginning of May, Wolfe confided in a letter to Pillsbury that he felt his chances for reconsideration were not good.[16] Some friends and at least two writers of letters to the newspapers urged Wolfe to answer the charges publicly; however, he held to his silence while there was the hope that the board might undo its action.

Prior to the June meeting, the regents received two letters, both dated June 10. One was from Jacob Wolfe, then serving as the commissioner of public lands in Nebraska. It consisted of a single sentence: "As a citizen of this state, and having, and taking a great pride and interest in the University and also as the father of H. K. Wolfe whom you have wisely or unwisely seen fit to depose from the Chair of Philosophy without assigning any reason therefor, I would respectfully ask that you give to me or the public your reason or reasons for said actions."[17] There was no response from the board of regents.

The second letter, six pages long, was written by Wolfe to address the causes of his dismissal "in so far as they have been made known to me."[18] The "intermeddling" charge apparently stemmed from an incident involving Wolfe and Hudson H. Nicholson, the head of the chemistry department, in the spring of 1896. As a member of the university's time card committee, which was responsible for verifying the accuracy of class enrollments and teaching assignments, Wolfe told Mac-Lean about what he believed was an exaggeration of enrollments in a report filed by Nicholson. The significance was that such figures were used as part of the formula for determining departmental budgets.

Nicholson was a powerful figure within the university. His chemistry building was the second structure to be built on the campus, opening in 1885. The following year he went to Europe on an equipment-buying trip for the new laboratory. He was the person in Nebraska most identified with the sugar beet industry. His work, through the agricultural experiment station, had been chiefly responsible for the industry's growth. Given Wolfe's continued frustration over support for his psychology laboratory, it would have been easy for him to be envious of Nicholson's success.[19]

Nicholson filed a second report, noting, "It has come to my attention that some individual with a talent for meddling—a modern Paul Pry with plenty of leisure for the indulgence of his unpleasant idiosyncrasy—has noted this fact [the error in counting students] and on it bases insinuations of fraud."[20] In his report, Nicholson explained how the error had been made, and the adjusted figures showed forty-three fewer students in his amended count.

Wolfe read Nicholson's amended report and then sent Mac-Lean a response indicating that he was not insinuating fraud

Lincoln, June 10, 1897

To the Honorable Board of Regents
University of Nebraska

Gentlemen,
Concerning the causes of
my removal, in so far as they have been
made known to me, I offer the following
statement.
"Intermeddling"
Near the beginning of each
semester the head of every department reports
to the executive office the *various courses*
given, the number of *hours of lectures* by
each instructor, the number of hours devoted by each instructor to *assistance in
laboratories*, and the *number of students*
in each course. The report made at
the

The first and last pages of Wolfe's June 10, 1897, letter to the board of regents regarding his dismissal from the University of Nebraska

but that there were still inaccuracies in Nicholson's report that should be investigated. For example, Wolfe noted that the course in advanced organic chemistry was exclusively a laboratory course. Yet on the reporting sheet, under the column for lecture or recitation, Nicholson had written "every day." According to Wolfe, it should have been left blank.[21]

It is not clear if Wolfe was correct in his accusations of errors in the reports from the chemistry department; however, the amended report filed by Nicholson suggests that Wolfe's arguments had some validity. It is certain that his "meddling" infuriated both Nicholson and MacLean. MacLean would later say that the regents had discussed this situation in 1896, perhaps at their April or June meetings, and that the regents had told

6

enough the professor whose report was corrected is said to agree with me on this point, and has also neglected to "coöperate". There are still other members of the Faculty who have been negligent in this matter.

"General Charges"
In the absence of any specific instances I deny the truth of the general charges which have been made in so far as they bear on the case under consideration.

I have never refused or neglected to obey an order or rule of the Regents or of the Chancellor or (wittingly) of the Faculty.

Very Respectfully
H. K. Wolfe

MacLean to warn Wolfe about further interference in the affairs of other departments. This was a warning that Wolfe said he had never received. And with or without the warning, Wolfe said he had dropped the matter during the previous year.[22] In his letter to the regents Wolfe claimed:

Since the beginning of the school year in September this matter has not been discussed, and when incidentally referred to was understood by me to be a case already settled. The investigation of the question seemed to me to be none of my business, the fact of a mistake in the report seemed to me to call for notification to the executive. I am not conscious of having "meddled" in any other affairs of any department.[23]

Wolfe also addressed the charge of noncooperation with the faculty. In the absence of any specificity, he was left to wonder what the charge could mean. He decided it referred to his refusal to report students for membership in Phi Beta Kappa, a practice that Nicholson followed as well. Wolfe, and other faculty members and students, had opposed the founding of a Phi Beta Kappa chapter on campus, calling it elitist. He told the regents: "As far as I know the Regents have never authorized the establishment of a chapter of this society or even recognized its existence. If they had done so, I, of course, would have complied with the requirements."[24]

If there was more to the charges than the affair with the chemistry department and the refusal to nominate students for Phi Beta Kappa, Wolfe was never to learn what that might be. He considered the possibility that his discharge might have been politically motivated, a thought he revealed to Pillsbury.[25] Several newspaper editors and letter writers also suggested a political reason for his firing. Wolfe's father had been chair of the Populist party in Nebraska, a party that had emerged largely as a result of farmers' dissatisfaction with the policies of both the Democrats and the Republicans. Jacob Wolfe had been elected Nebraska's commissioner of public lands on a Populist ticket that had captured the governor's office and several other important state positions. MacLean was a Republican, as were most of the members of the board of regents. It was argued that Wolfe's firing was retaliation for the Populist victories. After several newspaper editorials had implied such a political motive, the president of the board of regents, Charles H. Morrill, announced that the vote to dismiss Wolfe had been unanimous, including the two fusionist members of the board.[26]

The regents met on June 12 and 13 and, according to MacLean, discussed the letters from Wolfe and his father, yet they saw no reason to rescind their earlier decision.[27] Believing he had nothing to gain by continued silence, Wolfe released a lengthy letter to the press, giving his side of the story. It was his first public comment about his dismissal and was widely reprinted in Nebraska newspapers, including those in Lincoln and Omaha.[28]

Wolfe described his meeting with MacLean in which he had learned of the decision to dismiss him. He also gave his version of the incident with the chemistry department and his speculation that his stance on Phi Beta Kappa was the basis for the charge of "not cooperating with the faculty." He also attacked MacLean, describing several instances in which the chancellor had had open disagreements with the faculty. Wolfe painted him as a stubborn and authoritarian man who showed little regard for faculty members' opinions.

In addition, Wolfe described a meeting he had had with MacLean a few days before the regents were to meet in June. According to Wolfe's report, MacLean said to him: "You have said I am incompetent, insincere, and untruthful. You must first retract these statements as a basis for settlement between us."[29] If Wolfe made such statements about MacLean, they have not been found in print. Likely he felt that way about MacLean, and he may have shared his thoughts with others. Wolfe considered MacLean's statement to be evidence that his recommendation to the regents for Wolfe's dismissal was personally motivated.

During the last few weeks of June, the newspapers published a number of stories and letters related to Wolfe's dismissal. Several of these called on MacLean to respond to Wolfe's comments and to refute the charges if he could. A story in the *Lincoln Evening Post*, headlined "Cannot Remain Silent," was one of the most negative in its treatment of MacLean.

Chancellor MacLean is a man entirely unworthy of any man's confidence, much less the confidence of the state. . . . He cannot afford, relying upon the favor of the board of regents, to ignore these serious reflections upon his honesty and integrity. Such a course would destroy public pride and confidence in the university management, and he may well remember that there is a higher power than the board of regents.[30]

Yet MacLean did not reply, at least not until a newspaper reporter visited him on June 19.

By arrangement, a reporter for the *Evening Post* met MacLean at his home on the morning of the nineteenth. The interview ran on page one that evening. MacLean asserted that

Wolfe had been treated fairly and had been dismissed by a board of which MacLean was not a member. He added that he had always been kind to Wolfe and apparently Wolfe had taken this kindness as a sign that MacLean was "a fool or a sheepshead." When asked to answer Wolfe's published letter, MacLean responded:

> As an honorable man, with a reputation which has never been assailed, I do not feel that I can make any statement regarding the letter. Dr. Wolfe seemingly thinks that I am the one on trial and not he. In the letter there is nothing to which an honorable man in my position can reply. It deals with personalities and has not dealt with the real charges. It is not that I could not reply, but that I do not consider a reply necessary.[31]

In closing the interview, MacLean urged that the "useless agitation" cease. He warned, "Dr. Wolfe is the man who will suffer by its continuance."[32] MacLean was wrong about the letter's content. It was a lengthy account that dealt largely with the charges as Wolfe knew them; the treatment of "personalities" was a minor, albeit forceful, part of the letter.

On page two of that same issue of the newspaper was a story proposing Republican politics as the reason for Wolfe's dismissal.[33] It was a claim that would be repeated often in the next few months. Some Republican newspapers virtually admitted that the chancellor's action had been politically motivated, although they speculated that the regents may not have realized this and thus had based their vote on misinformation. However, if that were the case, the regents had an opportunity to reinstate Wolfe at their December 1897 meeting. At that meeting the regents discussed their political makeup, an odd occurrence because the board was supposed to be nonpartisan, and noted that two Populists were being added, causing the Republicans to lose one seat. In the context of that discussion, Wolfe's case was again raised. And once again the regents upheld their earlier action. Given the claims of political motives, it was an interesting juxtaposition of agenda items for the regents.[34]

Pressure on MacLean and the regents was considerable for many months after the announcement of Wolfe's firing. Letters poured into the university from former students and from the many teachers, principals, and parents around the state with whom Wolfe had worked in child study.[35] Newspaper editorials were sometimes vicious, especially those from Populist papers. Apparently, university students boycotted classes for a day, although reports are not clear about how many students actually participated. One seemingly far-fetched account said that MacLean had acted out of fear that Wolfe might replace him as chancellor.[36]

After the regents' December meeting, Wolfe and his supporters recognized that reinstatement was a lost cause. He was still unemployed, with no prospects for a job as yet. In fact, there is no indication that he had begun to apply for other positions at this time. He was so secure in his estimation of his value to the university and in the power of his supporters, and so confident of the lack of any real justification for dismissal, that he must have viewed it all as a horrible nightmare from which he would soon awaken. Thus the reality of the situation was slow to overtake him.

At the time of Wolfe's firing, MacLean was still new to his job as chancellor, having arrived in the fall term of 1895. He and Wolfe had clashed over several issues—Wolfe's overspending the departmental budget, teaching evolution, and questioning the accuracy of annual reports from other departments. It is easy to see how Wolfe's persistence and occasional self-righteousness would have caused problems for any administrator. Bessey and Canfield had endured it, admiring Wolfe's devotion to his students and recognizing what he was accomplishing. However, MacLean was not disposed to tolerate what he viewed as insubordination. Wolfe's ties to Populist politics may have been a factor, but it seems unlikely that MacLean needed that as a reason. When the opportunity arose, he got rid of a professor he saw as a troublemaker. And the regents, still in a honeymoon period with their chancellor, supported his wishes. The cries of "Wolfe! Wolfe! He's all right!" faded away—and Wolfe was gone.

Troubles continued for MacLean. In an 1898 meeting of the regents, a resolution supporting MacLean's accomplishments was not endorsed by several members of the board. Populist control of key state positions foretold that the party would soon gain control of the regents. And in 1900 it did, marking the first time the Republicans were in the minority in the history of the board of regents. MacLean might have been in serious trouble, except that he had seen the proverbial handwriting on the wall and had resigned the previous year to accept the presidency of the University of Iowa. Twelve years later, after alienating many members of his faculty and members of the Iowa legislature, he was dismissed from that post.[37]

For a year Wolfe was unemployed. Financial support for the family came from meager savings and from Katharine Wolfe's medical practice, a practice that she had resumed, after a six-year hiatus, when Isabel had begun school in 1895. At that time the Wolfes had moved to a large frame house at the corner of 14th and L streets in Lincoln. The house had a side door that led directly into Katharine's office and examining room. She enjoyed the work, and the extra money was helpful. When her husband lost his job, she took on extra patients, mostly women and children.

Wolfe used this time to analyze the data from experiments he had been conducting over the past several years. His teaching duties had occupied so much of his time that he had simply had no opportunity to prepare his studies for publication. Now he had plenty of time to write. The result was the publication of two lengthy monographs, one in the *American Journal of Psychology* and the other in the *Psychological Review*.[38]

Apparently Wolfe did not apply for any jobs until the summer of 1898, when he applied for three very diverse positions: the presidency of the University of Idaho, the chair in philosophy and education at the University of Washington, and the superintendency of the South Omaha Public Schools. His references for those jobs included former chancellor James Canfield, G. Stanley Hall, E. B. Titchener, and William Jennings Bryan. Wolfe accepted his only offer, a three-year contract to take charge of the schools in South Omaha.

South Omaha was a municipality separate from Omaha at the turn of the century (it would be annexed to the larger city in 1915). It was a community on the wrong side of the tracks, a town that had grown up around the railroads and the smells of the stockyards and the packing plants that had located there in the latter part of the nineteenth century. Its 1890 population of eight thousand had jumped to twenty-six thousand by 1900. At the time of Wolfe's arrival in 1898, the packing plants employed more than four thousand workers, most of whom lived in South Omaha.[39] In addition to its packing industry, the city was known for its many saloons. John B. Carns, a Methodist minister from Grand Island and the first superintendent of Nebraska's Anti-Saloon League, called South Omaha Nebraska's "worst city."[40]

Compared with Omaha, it was a poor city. Its populace regularly endured derision from the social-class sophisticates of the larger city to the north. Education was said to be important in this community of fierce pride, yet schools were woefully funded, attendance was poor, and dropping out was common practice for students. Some citizens felt that hiring Wolfe would provide the impetus for a much-needed educational reform.

Drawing on his background in the child study groups, Wolfe met with parents in neighborhood and church groups to ask for their help in getting their children to attend school. At two campuses, he established night schools for adult students. He appealed especially to those recent dropouts who needed only a few credits to graduate. He staffed these schools with some of his best teachers, using them half days in the regular classes and adding salary bonuses for their night work.

Wolfe was particularly concerned about the science curriculum and the scientific preparation of many of the teachers. He established a program for science education for teachers, offering incentives for them to take summer classes. He persuaded the school board to appropriate funds for laboratory equipment, including microscopes.

Not all of Wolfe's "progressive" ideas were well received, however. His placement of Greek statues, with fig leaves intact, at some of the schools drew some negative comments from parts of the citizenry. Visitors to his superintendent's office were treated to a display of much statuary and prints of many famous European paintings, mostly acquired when he was a student in Germany.[41] Similarly, he was criticized for providing the school libraries with books that featured stories about people who lived in caves, thus drawing attacks about the teaching of evolution.

Despite these few incidents, reaction to Wolfe was generally positive. School attendance improved, dropout rates decreased, new night schools had to be added because of demand, and teacher morale was said to have improved. Yet Wolfe, perhaps recalling his budget frustrations at the University of Nebraska, found it impossible to get the resources he felt he needed. Almost from the day he took the job, he began to lobby for a new high school building. The current one was in such terrible shape that Wolfe believed it contributed to the dropout problem. Each year the issue was put to a vote of the school board and each year it failed. Money was an issue for South Omaha schools; for example, Wolfe received an eighteen-hundred-dollar salary during his third year as superintendent, whereas his counterpart in Omaha, Carroll G. Pearse, received thirty-six hundred dollars.[42]

Toward the end of Wolfe's third year in South Omaha, he made the decision not to seek another term. The reasons for that decision are not clear. His letters indicate that he felt he would have been reelected by the board but not on his own terms. Those terms are not identified. It seems unlikely that the issue of a new high school building was the sole reason for such a decision; however, that issue may have been symptomatic of the board's lack of support in several other areas.

In the spring of 1901, Wolfe applied for the superintendent's job in the Sioux City, Iowa, schools but was unsuccessful. When the school term ended in early summer, with Isabel finishing the eighth grade, the Wolfes moved back to the family farm at Normal. The furniture was put in storage in Lincoln. And Wolfe was unemployed once again.

Wolfe, who had always fancied himself a farmer, decided to raise chickens. He bought an incubator, which was placed next to his mother's piano in the parlor. When all the young chicks got roup, a poultry disease, Katharine, perhaps because of her medical degree, was given the task of swabbing hundreds of tiny throats. The chicks recovered and were well on their way to being placed in coops, which Wolfe had built. However, someone let the incubator temperature rise too much, and one hundred chicks were roasted prematurely. That incident marked the end of the chicken business for the Wolfes.[43]

While raising his chickens, Wolfe learned of an opening in the Department of Pedagogy at New York University (NYU) for the chair in experimental psychology. The vacancy was created when Charles H. Judd (1873–1946), also one of Wundt's students, and two other professors resigned in protest over the administration of the department.[44] Wolfe, perhaps in desperation to return to a university job, had thirteen letters of reference sent to the university's chancellor. James Canfield, then the librarian at Columbia University, wrote a very glowing letter in which he offered to meet with the NYU chancellor if it would help Wolfe's chances. The current chancellor of the University of Nebraska, Benjamin Andrews, was also one of the letter writers, noting that Wolfe had a "quite uncommon power to draw pupils to his work and to himself." However, the job went to Robert MacDougall of Harvard University.[45]

Wolfe applied for the presidency of a state normal school and was unsuccessful, as he was in his application for the chair in philosophy at the University of Washington, the second time he had applied for that position. Certainly one of the factors against Wolfe for the faculty positions was his age. He was forty-four and the university jobs were going to "younger men." Indeed his age was raised as an issue when he was being considered for a position at the University of California at Berkeley in the summer of 1902.[46] Further, there is no doubt that universities worried about the circumstances of Wolfe's departure from the University of Nebraska. The former Nebraska chancellor Charles Bessey addressed the personality question in his letter of reference to the president of the University of Washington. "Personally you will find him a very pleasant man. He has strong opinions, and is frank and fearless in expressing them, and this has led some people to imagine that he is hard to get on with, but I know from long personal experience that it is merely his strong way of stating his full convictions."[47]

Finally, in July 1902, Wolfe got a job, one for which he did not apply. The family moved back to Lincoln, renting a house on G Street, and got the furniture out of storage. In the fall, Wolfe began the new school year as the principal of Lincoln High School, at a salary of two thousand dollars. In making the selection, the Lincoln Board of Education had considered a number of distinguished applicants. Wolfe's name had surfaced when the board had received several letters from alumni of the school who had studied with Wolfe at the university and from some of his former colleagues there.

The high school was a large one, enrolling nearly twelve hundred students at the time of Wolfe's arrival. The building, designed for a maximum enrollment of eight hundred, was woefully small for such a large group. Virtually every room was in use as a classroom. Many classrooms were described as dingy, cramped, dark, and wholly unsuited for learning. Not surprisingly, Wolfe once again found himself in a campaign for a new school building.[48] As a short-term measure for beautification, Wolfe spent over four hundred dollars to purchase prints of classic paintings. These were framed and hung in a number of rooms in the building. Yet their role was more than mere decoration. Drawing on the ideas of John Amos Comenius (1592–1670), a Moravian educator and theologian who had emphasized the use of visual illustrations in teaching, Wolfe argued, "[Pictures] keep before our minds great ideas, worthy lives and deeds, wonderful and beautiful products of imagination and skill." Wolfe placed classic paintings in the schoolrooms because "the influence of frequent contemplation of the best works of art" was "inestimable."[49]

One of Wolfe's first acts was to establish a system of self-government for the students, giving them greater responsibility for their conduct. Controversial at first, the procedure seemed to work well, with noted improvement in student behavior in the classrooms, halls, and auditorium assemblies.

Special help was offered to students who were having academic problems. Students who received two or more Ds on exams were required to come to school an hour early and stay an extra two hours after school for tutoring. The percentage of failing grades declined dramatically. That may have been the result of the tutoring, or perhaps it was due to additional studying by students who wanted to avoid the extra three hours of school each day.[50]

Near the conclusion of Wolfe's second year at Lincoln High School, a second daughter, Katharine Alice, was born. Isabel was then fourteen, and her mother and father were thirty-eight and forty-five respectively. Katharine Alice was actually the third child born to the Wolfes. A son, Sidney, was born in 1892 but died at the age of eighteen months when he was fatally burned by a bowl of hot jelly that he pulled off a shelf where it had been left to cool. The accident occurred in California when Katharine was visiting a friend.

After the death of Sidney, Katharine wanted to have another child, but Wolfe objected, perhaps because of his fears of suffering another loss. Katharine acceded to his wishes for ten years before she decided to get pregnant again, and Katharine Alice was born. And then later, in early 1908, she gave birth to a son, Harry, the last child of her "second" family, a family that her husband welcomed despite his earlier reluctance.[51]

With their new daughter, the Wolfes moved from the rental house, purchasing a small home near the high school. Wolfe's job was going well, and he was praised by parents, teachers, students, and the board of education for his accomplishments. In fact, there was fear in the community that he would leave, especially when Pearse left his post as superintendent of the Omaha schools. The Omaha school board announced they were considering Wolfe, although Pearse, in a parting comment, cautioned, "While Wolfe is a very able man he has not sufficient diplomacy to fill the position of superintendent of the Omaha schools."[52]

Lincoln's fears were realized during the 1904–5 school year when Wolfe received an invitation from the University of Montana. Wolfe was eager to return to a university post but reluctant to leave Lincoln, a city to which he was deeply attached. The attractions of a move to Missoula included the fact that his sister Jessie lived there; her husband was the superintendent of the Missoula schools. Most important, though, was the nature of the position—professor of philosophy and pedagogy. In a letter to Wolfe, the president of the University of Montana described Wolfe's duties. "Your special work is expected to be in the lines of Psychology and Pedagogy. I think it probable that we shall want you to go out from the university from time to time as instructor in teacher's institutes."[53] The only job description that could have sounded better to Wolfe would have been a similar offer from the University of Nebraska.

The salary offer at Montana was no more than his principal's salary, two thousand dollars. The offer was made with the understanding that Wolfe would be able to begin in midyear, starting at the resumption of classes in January 1905. So Wolfe had the unpleasant tasks of leaving Lincoln High School on short notice and moving Isabel in the middle of her senior year. Bessey wrote to Wolfe on Christmas Eve, congratulating him on the Montana position but lamenting the loss for the city of Lincoln.[54] Wolfe arrived in Missoula shortly after the Christmas holidays. The rest of his family stayed behind for another six weeks while Katharine Alice recovered from scarlet fever.

Wolfe was once again teaching university students about the new psychology and its applications to pedagogy. In the summer of 1905 he was involved in a series of three-day workshops held around the state and offered by the extension program of the University of Montana. At each of these he gave two lectures, one on "Applied Psychology" and a second entitled "Knowledge of Children."[55] In the fall, Wolfe began his second semester of teaching. Isabel, bewitched by the mountains, had enrolled in the university. Then, shortly after the beginning of the fall term, events began to unfold in Lincoln—events that would bring Wolfe's Montana days to an end.

In September, F. W. Smith, an adjunct professor of education at the University of Nebraska, announced his resignation to accept the presidency of a normal school in Paterson, New Jersey. Luckey acted quickly. He wrote to Chancellor Benjamin Andrews, describing the teaching needs of the education department and asking that the part-time position be made into a full-time job. Not surprisingly, Luckey said he knew just the person to fill such a position. In fact, Luckey had already written to Wolfe about the position. Luckey had nine hundred dollars unencumbered in his budget and proposed it as a one-semester salary for Wolfe. He told Andrews that he had communicated with Wolfe and that Wolfe had agreed to come for nine hundred dollars for the spring semester and for a salary of two thousand dollars beginning the next fall. Chancellor Andrews wrote to Wolfe in October, offering him a position as professor of educational psychology, under the terms Luckey had described.[56] Wolfe replied a few days later, accepting the offer and expressing his appreciation to Andrews for his help in bringing Wolfe back to Nebraska.[57]

Thus Wolfe's tenure at Montana was a year, actually two halves of two separate academic years. Although he was at Montana for only a short period of time, he made a considerable impact on the students there. The *Missoula Standard* reported his departure.

[Wolfe] left tonight on the Burlington for his new field of labor. At the train he was given a rousing sendoff by the students, who were at the train in large numbers to bid him adieu as he left for the east. The members of his classes, in recognition of his services to them, presented him at the train with a solid silver dish, of handsome pattern and suitably engraved. They speak of him in the highest praise as a teacher and regret exceedingly that he has left. . . . The students of his classes passed resolutions speaking in the highest terms of his work with them, a copy of which was presented to him at the train this evening.[58]

That send-off marked quite a display of affection and admiration for a professor who had spent only a year at the University of Montana and who was leaving in the middle of the school year.

The *Omaha World Herald* welcomed Wolfe home with an editorial entitled "A Blot Wiped Out."[59] Perhaps most important, many of his friends at the University of Nebraska held a special homecoming for him. One of those who welcomed him was Thaddeus Lincoln Bolton, a psychologist who had studied with Hall at Clark University. Bolton had joined the Nebraska faculty in 1900 and occupied Wolfe's old position as chair of the Department of Philosophy. Bolton taught most of the psychology courses and had added two courses to the psychology curriculum, one entitled "Animal Psychology" and a second entitled "Child Psychology." Hinman was still a member of the faculty, carrying most of the philosophy load. He shared philosophy classes with a third faculty member, Ferdinand C. French, who had come to Nebraska from Colgate University. French, who also taught a course in social psychology, was the same French who in the 1890s had taken issue with Wolfe's claim for the appropriateness of laboratory work in psychology for undergraduate students.[60]

Wolfe was housed in the College of Education, essentially sharing the duties in pedagogy with his close friend Luckey. He taught classes in educational psychology, child study, and school management. Wolfe and Luckey worked well together, and the success of their programs attracted even more students to an already overburdened teacher-training curriculum.[61]

In 1908, at the close of Wolfe's second year in the College of Education, Bolton was dismissed by Chancellor Andrews, who was leaving the university. Bolton asked for a statement of the specific charges against him, yet no charges were forthcoming from the administration. It was well known that he and Andrews did not get along with one another. Their tension had come to a head when Andrews had reneged on a promise for more space for the psychology laboratory. Based on correspondence and Bolton's annual reports, it appears Bolton was as determined as Wolfe had been to improve the laboratory, and for a while it seemed he would be more successful. After considerable lobbying from Bolton, the administration promised him seven rooms in the new physics building, scheduled for completion in 1905. He proudly described his new laboratory-to-be in an article, "The Changing Attitude of American Universities Toward Psychology," published in *Science*.[62] However, several months later the University of Nebraska, showing it had not changed its attitude, reassigned the rooms to the physics department. Bolton protested vehemently, but to no avail. The administration offered him several rooms in the basement of the administration building, rooms he declared less suitable than his current space.[63]

This affair must have looked painfully familiar to Wolfe. When the new chancellor, Samuel Avery, took over, Bolton asked for a hearing on his dismissal, but Avery refused to reopen his case. And so Bolton, who had a reputation as an excellent teacher, was dismissed. He accepted a position at the normal school in Tempe, Arizona (later Arizona State University). In the year that followed, Wolfe remained in the College of Education; however, he taught several of Bolton's courses, including experimental and genetic psychology.

In the fall of 1909, Wolfe assumed his old position as professor and chair of the Department of Philosophy, joining Hinman and French. Likely there was some tension between French and Wolfe. The former had been under some pressure earlier because of negative comments from students about his teaching. Rumors circulated that French had left Vassar College because of students' dissatisfaction. Although the reason is not clear, French resigned from the University of Nebraska in April 1910, returning to Colgate. His departure allowed Wolfe to hire his former student Hartley Burr Alexander, an 1897 Nebraska graduate. Alexander had completed his doctorate in philosophy at Columbia University in 1901, where he had studied with Cattell. Yet Alexander's interests were chiefly in philosophy, rather than psychology. He did help with the psychology curriculum, adding a course entitled "Suggestion and Psychotherapy," the first clinically related course to be a part of the university's curriculum in psychology.

As psychology enrollments continued to climb, Wolfe needed more help on that side of the department. In 1915 he hired Winifred Florence Hyde, who, like Alexander, had been an undergraduate at Nebraska, earning her baccalaureate in 1900. Hyde had received her doctorate in philosophy from Jena University in Germany, the first woman to earn a doctoral degree from that institution.[64]

Wolfe's second period of employment at the University of Nebraska was largely a successful and happy one. He conducted very little of his own research during this period, yet he spent much of his time supervising students' projects. He maintained close ties to Nebraska's teachers and was a frequent speaker at their meetings. He kept up his efforts to improve the psychology laboratory in terms of space and equipment, and finally, in 1917, he was authorized by Chancellor Avery to design his dream laboratory as part of a new social sciences building.

Wolfe's father, Jacob, and Wolfe's three children: Harry, Isabel, and Katharine (ca. 1910)

Wolfe watched Isabel graduate from the University of Nebraska with baccalaureate and master's degrees. He witnessed her marriage in 1914 to Ansel Hemenway, a professor of biology at Transylvania University in Kentucky. He greatly enjoyed his younger children, his "second family," and Isabel's two children as well. In short, his family life was a source of much pleasure.

In the meantime, war clouds were gathering in Europe. Soon they would reach Nebraska, plunging the university into its darkest hours. The tranquility of Wolfe's life was about to be shattered.

Chapter Six

Patriotism
on Trial

America in 1914 was enjoying considerable prosperity on the heels of the second industrial revolution. The new industries of chemicals, electricity, oil, and steel not only had added to the ranks of America's millionaires but also had significantly enlarged the middle class. Large migrations to the cities continued, emphasizing the political and social influence of the cities. Nationally, debate centered on the issues of Prohibition and woman suffrage, issues that were part of Nebraska political campaigns as well. However, Nebraska, still chiefly agrarian, focused much of its attention on farm issues, such as the federally funded agricultural extension programs provided by the Smith-Lever Act of 1914.

Much of America seemed ill prepared for the outbreak of war in Europe in the summer of 1914. Economically, some of the country underwent an initial recession due to the loss of commerce with Europe, but that changed quickly as orders for war supplies came from the Allies. Of paramount importance was food, and in that regard Nebraska reaped a bonanza. Between 1915 and 1916, prices for Nebraska crops doubled: wheat rose from 84¢ a bushel to $1.60, corn from 47¢ a bushel to 78¢, and potatoes from 42¢ a bushel to $1.50. Not surprisingly, the war years brought even greater prosperity to the state.[1]

But for some Nebraska citizens, principally its German-Americans, the war in Europe was a time of intense persecution. Questions of patriotism gave vent to deep-seated prejudices, and a number of people suffered from accusations of disloyalty. Wolfe was among that number. His education in Germany, his wife's roots in that country, and his views on patriotism led him to actions that resulted in his being brought to trial in 1918 along with more than a dozen of his university colleagues. The *Aurora Republican* referred to this group as "invertebrate Americans" and was one of many Nebraska newspapers that called for the University of Nebraska to "clean its house."[2]

At the outbreak of the war, German-Americans represented a sizable portion of the population of the United States. In Nebraska, they were the single largest ethnic group, according to the 1910 census: 20 percent of the state's inhabitants were of German origin, and among the foreign-born in the state, and their children, 50 percent originated from Germany. In 1910 they formed the German-American Alliance, an organization of local chapters that sought to preserve some aspects of German culture and to unify their political efforts in Nebraska. Most of the chapters, or lodges, were formed around religious interests, principally Lutheran but also Protestant and Roman Catholic. Some chapters were linked by common cultural goals, rather than religious interests. Thus considerable diversity existed within the Alliance, often hindering the organization's effectiveness. But to most outsiders, the Alliance appeared to be a rather homogeneous group.[3]

Anti-German feelings clearly existed in America before the war. Although most Americans argued for American neutrality when war broke out, they were also quick to side with the Allies against the nation they viewed as the aggressor. Anti-German sentiment reached new heights. Nevertheless, many German-Americans, disparagingly referred to as "hyphenated Americans," sought to defend the actions of their distant homeland, where most had relatives, some of whom were directly involved in the fighting.[4] Organized efforts were launched to counteract the "lies" about Germany being reported by the Allies and echoed in the American press. Some of the most vocal proponents for Germany's cause came from within the universities, the most notable example being Hugo Münsterberg of Harvard University.

Münsterberg, a native of Danzig, retained his German citizenship throughout his residency in America. A psychologist who had earned his doctorate with Wundt in 1885, a year earlier than Wolfe, Münsterberg became the self-appointed spokesperson for Germany's cause. As a psychologist, he had always been "good copy" because of his interest in many applied topics and his penchant for the sensational.[5] Now he turned his efforts to writing newspaper and magazine articles and books as part of his propaganda effort. In 1914 he wrote a letter, printed in the *Boston Herald* and reprinted widely, in which he explained the war as an "inevitable clash between the forces of civilization, represented by Teutonic Germany, and the forces of barbarism, headed by Slavic Russia."[6] His activities caused him turmoil in Boston and on his campus; in October 1914 he stopped attending faculty meetings. Yet his war work continued. He even began to work secretly with a German propaganda cabinet that had been organized by the German embassy and that met weekly in New York City. When the *Lusitania* was sunk by a German submarine in 1915, his faith in the German cause was seriously shaken. He turned his efforts to psychology once again, this time in virtual isolation.[7]

The sinking of the *Lusitania* marked a significant change in German-American political activities. More efforts were now focused on ways to maintain U.S. neutrality and less on vocal support of Germany. Woodrow Wilson, the incumbent president, campaigned in 1916 to keep America out of the war. Although hardly neutral, he was regarded as a pacifist. In the fall of 1916, the German-Americans in Lincoln formed a "Wilson Club," supporting his reelection as the best of several bad choices.[8] On April 6, 1917, a month after beginning his second term, Wilson called for and got a declaration of war. The hard times for German-Americans were about to get much worse.

In Nebraska, in 1916, the governor's race was under way. In the Democratic primary, the German-American Alliance gave strong support to Keith Neville, a candidate opposed to Prohibition. His opponent, Charles W. Bryan, the younger brother of William Jennings Bryan, supported Prohibition.[9] Neville won, but the state voted to go dry in the same election. By May 1917, the Nebraska legislature had made Prohibition the law.

On April 18, twelve days after the declaration of war, Governor Neville established the Nebraska State Council of Defense, modeled on the National Council of Defense, to coordinate Nebraska's war efforts. The twelve-member council included the governor and was headed by a Lincoln hardware-store owner, Robert M. Joyce. The secret service committee of the council, charged with investigating disloyal activities, was headed by Richard L. Metcalfe, an Omaha newspaper editor. By July 1917, less than three months after the council was formed, it notified the University of Nebraska that several of its professors were "out of harmony with the American cause" and suggested that appropriate action be taken.[10]

Despite the letter from the council and some additional prodding in the local newspapers, the university did not act on the charges, at least not in any public manner. Perhaps this inaction resulted from bureaucratic inertia; more likely it stemmed from Chancellor Samuel Avery's belief that the charges of disloyalty were unfounded. He argued that although the accused professors might be guilty of idealism in international affairs, they had eventually come to understand the folly of their pacifism.

Samuel Avery, an agricultural chemist, had moved up from the faculty ranks in the university to become its chancellor in 1909. His doctoral degree had been earned at the University of Heidelberg, and he was on record as an admirer of German *kultur*. In a 1910 speech at a German-American rally in Lincoln, Avery had said: "For two years I was an academic Burger of Heidelberg. My legal protector was the noble Friedrich, grand duke of Baden, and I had every right of a citizen of that country. The proudest academic distinction that I ever won was granted me in his name."[11] Such remarks were acceptable in 1910, but they would later haunt Avery, affecting the way he dealt with the accusations of disloyalty within his faculty.

The conflict at the university began with two telegrams sent to President Wilson. The first, sent on April 1, 1917, expressed unqualified support for the president and stated that opposition to the war was "untimely and dangerous." Avery was among the seventy-three signers of this telegram. The second telegram, sent the next day, was signed by eighty-nine employees of the university. Wolfe's name occupied the fifth position on the petition. Referred to as the "peace petition," it asked that the federal government content itself "with preparations for defense and measures calculated to defend our commerce and that it use all honorable means of preventing American aggressive participation in the present European conflict." The entire text of the second telegram was published in the *Nebraska State Journal* on April 10, four days after war was declared, and included the names of the signers. The article quoted from a follow-up letter written by the signers and stating, "It is of course to be understood that all the signers are now ready to support the president and congress in their conduct of the war."[12]

Avery followed on April 14 with a speech that he hoped would bring the matter to a close, announcing that although some faculty had been slower than others to recognize the justness and necessity of the war, all were now united in their support of the government. But the matter would not go away. It was kept alive by newspaper editors, such as Metcalfe, who objected to young people being exposed to instructors who were labeled wishy-washy at best or cowards at worst; by the council, spurred in part by Metcalfe's efforts there; and by several members of the university's faculty who were incensed by the lack of patriotism shamefully displayed by some of their colleagues. Two faculty members were conspicuously active in supplying the council with accusations about their colleagues. One was Minnie England, an assistant professor of economics, and the other was Fred Morrow Fling, a professor of history and the more zealous and self-righteous of the two.

Fling had earned his doctorate in Leipzig in 1890 with a dissertation on the Comte de Mirabeau's role in the French Revolution. Fling was a strong supporter of the French and an early critic of Wilson's pacifism and of any American who offered "excuses for the Hun." His outspokenness earned him a reprimand from the university in 1914 but did not seem to dampen his ardor in pointing his patriotic finger at those he judged to be disloyal. He would be a significant figure in the hearings to come. [13]

Some historians have referred to the spring of 1918 in the United States as America's "reign of terror." It was a time "when strident voices filled the air, when mobs swarmed through the streets, when violence of all kinds was practiced upon the opponents of the war." Some of the violence came in the form of laws, enacted by state legislatures or by the numerous state and local councils of defense. In Nebraska, the legislature passed a law in 1917 prohibiting non-U.S. citizens from teaching in the public and parochial schools of the state. During the winter of 1917–18 there was a national movement to abolish the teaching of the German language in schools, a move that was supported by people such as Theodore Roosevelt and by groups such as the state councils of defense. In a *New York Times* editorial in 1918, Knight Dunlap, a distinguished professor of psychology at Johns Hopkins University, added his voice to the movement, pronouncing the German language a "barbarous tongue lacking in cultural worth and without commercial importance." [14]

In December 1917, the Nebraska State Council of Defense asked the legislature for a ban on the use of the German language in all Nebraska schools, an action that would have had serious consequences for many of the Lutheran schools in particular, some of which conducted all classes in German for the children of recent immigrants. A law prohibiting teaching in a language other than English was debated in the Nebraska legislature during 1918 and eventually passed in 1919 (the law was declared unconstitutional by the United States Supreme Court in 1923). [15]

Teachers, at all levels, were objects of scrutiny. Before the declaration of war, many had spoken out against American involvement. They had been active in peace activities such as pacifist parades. But now that the United States was involved, "they either supported the war enthusiastically or kept quiet." Indeed, schools had become "seminaries of patriotism"; many of them initiated military training programs where none had existed before. The American Defense Society was one of several national and state organizations to support the establishment of a mandatory teacher's oath of patriotic support, but the war ended before a federal law could be enacted.[16]

War fervor grew as the local papers daily documented the names of the Nebraskans who had died abroad. In January 1918, the State Council of Defense renewed its efforts to prod the university into action. Governor Neville strongly supported the council's action, noting that university professors needed to realize that during the war there could be "no such thing as academic freedom."[17] Still, there was no formal action from the university, partly because the president of the board of regents, Frank Haller, defended the accused on the grounds of academic freedom and argued that an overzealous council had misunderstood its mission by initiating such a witch hunt. However, the council persisted in its accusations toward the university.

On April 19, 1918, the council sent a two-page letter to each member of the board of regents and to the newspapers. In part it read:

> During the past ten months many reports and complaints have reached the State Council of Defense, with regard to the un-American attitude of persons connected with the University. Some of these reports show a decidedly pro-German sympathy; others an attitude of mind wholly out of harmony with the supreme purpose of the nation in its war work. . . .
>
> These are days when every one connected with the State University should be measured absolutely by an active, outspoken fealty to the nation, and that notions of academic freedom which permits or excuses lack of wholehearted aggressive support of the nation at this critical time, should be severely frowned upon and dealt with.
>
> Nebraska's leading educational institution should and must be one hundred per cent agressively [sic] American. Behavior which is negative, halting or hesitating by anyone on the University staff, in support of the government, should not be tolerated and especially all teaching which is covertly insidious in its influence upon the minds of students should be made impossible.
>
> The boards of many universities and colleges of the

country have taken vigorous action to purge themselves
of such pernicious influences and on behalf of the patriotic
people of the University and state we ask you to do like-
wise in support of the government.
　　We trust instant action will be taken in regard to this
matter.[18]

The council was correct in its assertion of actions at other universities. Dismissals of faculty members for disloyalty, sedition, lack of sufficient patriotism, and other charges were occurring from coast to coast.[19]

Among the many dismissed were a couple of eminent, or
soon-to-be eminent, psychologists. Edward Chace Tolman
(1886–1959), a young instructor at Northwestern University,
was fired on the grounds of war retrenchment and poor teaching, but he believed he was dismissed for his pacifist views,
some of which had been published in a pacifist newspaper.[20]
Undoubtedly, the most famous case involved Columbia University's firing of James McKeen Cattell, Wolfe's fellow graduate student at Leipzig and arguably the most famous American
psychologist at that time. Cattell was dismissed in October
1917 by the trustees of Columbia after they evaluated complaints received from several members of Congress; in letters
written to the members, Cattell had objected to sending
draftees to fight in Europe.[21]

The Nebraska council's letter of April 19 to the regents did
not name names, but it did name two units as problematic: the
Graduate School of Education and the Department of American History. When the item appeared in the *Lincoln Daily Star*
that day, the newspaper noted that Professors George W. A.
Luckey and Clark Edmund Persinger headed those two units.
The *Star*, one of the newspapers most vocally in support of the
council's inquiries, called for a probe that would identify the
professors who were "patriotic idlers."[22]

The regents met on April 24 to discuss the council's letter,
and they replied to the council by letter the following day. The
regents argued that they were reluctant to act on what they
deemed anonymous complaints and called for the council to
provide specific charges. The regents also indicated their desire for a public hearing in which the accused would have the

opportunity to defend themselves. Further, the regents suggested that the council serve as prosecutor in such a hearing.[23]

The council released the letter to the press and joined with the press in a continued bombardment of the university. A story in the *Lincoln Daily Star* on April 26 quoted the council as having already turned over specific charges on one faculty member and as possessing "a quantity of sworn affidavits and letters" implicating other professors.[24]

At its next meeting, on May 17, the council approved a seven-page letter to be sent to the regents along with the mass of supporting documents the council had collected. The council chastised the regents for continuing to drag their feet and especially for the regents' suggestion that the council conduct the hearings. Concerning that issue, the council wrote:

Responsibility of this character does not rest alone with the State Council. Immediately it rests with the men in authority in any public institution and a mere suggestion of an undesirable situation ought to be sufficient to command immediate action on the part of those in authority. The facts are so readily accessible to your board that very little effort on your part will remove all cause for complaint. Official boards in other universities have remedied the evils in their institutions and there appears to be no reason why the official board of the University of Nebraska should not act with similar energy in the discharge of its plain duty. The work of the State Council is so large and its duties so manifold that it has the right to expect that organizations like yours will correct bad conditions in the business immediately entrusted to them without seeking to place the State Council in the role of prosecutor.[25]

The bulk of the letter described specific examples of reprehensible behavior by twelve university employees. None of the accused were named in the letter; however, their names did appear in the supporting documents, which consisted of letters and affidavits. Some of these documents had been sent directly to the council by concerned citizens, and others had been deliberately gathered by the council, often acting on information it received about a particular person. After the presentation of the specific incidents, the council added: "Apart from the direct evidence which we herewith present, you have a right, and it is your duty, to make inquiry as to a generally unsatisfactory condition on this point. To this end we suggest that if your board does not already know what has been going on to the detriment of America that you make inquiry of the following named distinguished Nebraskans."[26]

Thirteen names followed, four of which were associated with the university: Samuel Avery, who was on leave with a wartime assignment in Washington, D.C.; Acting Chancellor William Hastings; Langworthy Taylor, a professor of economics; and Fred Fling. Of those four, Fling had been the most helpful in supplying the council with information damaging to his colleagues. In concluding its letter, the council wrote, "In the discharge of our duty to have pointed out the cancer in the University of Nebraska and in the name of the people of this state we call upon you to take immediate action."[27]

The council sent the letter to the regents on May 20, releasing it to the press at the same time; however, the press did not receive the supporting documents that identified the twelve who were accused. Some of the accused surely must have recognized themselves in the specificity of the incidents described in the newspapers. Yet others must have wondered if they were among the twelve: some incidents were described in such general terms that the council may have been referring to any of the eighty-nine university employees who had signed the peace petition. Speculation about the identity of the twelve was the talk of the campus and the broader Lincoln community.

The regents met on May 25 to discuss the council's latest letter. That afternoon they agreed to mail copies of the charges, along with the supporting affidavits and letters, to each of the twelve accused. The information was provided so that the accused could prepare their defenses. The regents agreed to hold public hearings beginning on May 28. Thus the defendants had approximately forty-eight hours to prepare.[28]

The names were made public in the *Lincoln Daily Star* on the day the hearings began. The headline indicated that twelve were accused, but the newspaper listed only eleven; the charges against a professor of German had been withdrawn before the hearings began. Of the eleven, all were faculty members, with one exception—a woman who served as the secretary of the alumni association. Ten of the eleven, plus the professor whose charges were dismissed, had signed the April 2, 1917, peace petition. Persinger was on the list, as was Luckey. So was Howard Caldwell, who had graduated from the university with Wolfe in 1880. There had been some speculation earlier that Wolfe would be among the twelve accused, but he was not.[29]

The chief attorney, H. H. Wilson—a law professor at the university and the husband of Emma Parks, Wolfe's only female classmate in his graduating class—was appointed by the regents. In his acceptance letter to the board, Wilson indicated that he had hoped the assignment would go to someone else. He followed that statement with some flag waving. "When, however, our boys are . . . risking their lives in the great cause, I appreciate that it is no time for anyone else to fail to heed the call of duty." Lastly he added some comments about his fairness and his malice toward none.[30]

Wilson also suggested a list of eight principles and procedures for the hearings, to which the board agreed. One of these noted that the proceedings did not constitute a criminal proceeding. Wilson said his job was to present all of the relevant information, both the positive and negative, on each case. A second principle stated, "The charge is disloyalty and the acts and language specified will be treated merely as evidence of disloyalty." A third point emphasized the fact that the integrity of the university had been called into question by the necessity of these hearings. Wilson urged the board to demonstrate the university's commitment to a thorough investigation. He suggested, "Invite all patriotic organizations and the public in general to bring forward any evidence they may possess touching disloyalty in the University, even where the same might involve members of the faculty, instructors, or employees not mentioned in the charges before the board."[31]

The hearings, held in the Law Building on the campus, began the morning of May 28. Members of the board of regents presided over the hearings, chaired by Edward P. Brown, the recently elected chair of the regents. Newspapers reported

The trial room in the Law Building held capacity crowds each day for the "Disloyalty Hearings" in the summer of 1918. (Photo courtesy of the Nebraska Historical Society)

that the room was packed for most of the hearings and that many women were in attendance. A photograph of the hearing confirms that description, showing more than one hundred people in attendance, many of them wearing their broad-brimmed bonnets. Most of the first day of hearings dealt with the cases of Luckey and Caldwell. They were two of Wolfe's closest friends on the faculty. Indeed, the children of Wolfe, Luckey, and Caldwell were frequent companions.

The next day, the first person not on the original list of twelve was called before the board to answer charges against him—it was Wolfe. Headlines in the *Lincoln Daily Star* on May 29 read, "PROF. WOLFE, NOT ON COUNCIL LIST, BEFORE REGENTS." The charges against him had been initiated by the council's secret service committee; it was alleged that Wolfe had refused to sign a card indicating his subscriptions to various wartime activities. The council had also received a letter, signed "A Taxpayer," that accused Wolfe of expressing pro-German views in his classes and of arguing for the validity of the German educational system.[32]

It is not known how much advance notice Wolfe received about his day in court. The board had stated that those called during the course of the hearings would be given notice sufficient to allow them to prepare their defense. However, because he was not among the original twelve, who got only forty-eight hours' notice, and because he testified on the morning of the second day of the hearings, it is likely that Wolfe had very little, if any, time to prepare.

The hearing opened that morning with the charges being read to Wolfe: that he had not signed a wartime activity subscription card, that he had not displayed a Red Cross emblem in his office or home, and that when he had made a donation to the Red Cross Fund, he had asked that his name not be recorded. Wolfe answered these charges in his opening statement, indicating that he had not known he was supposed to sign the card and stating that it was not his habit to do so. He had no recollection of refusing to sign such a card, nor did he remember refusing to display a Red Cross emblem. No one had asked him to do so, and again, he said, such displays were not in his normal behavior. He had made his Red Cross donation through a friend at the university and had asked that it be made anonymously. It was not that he did not support the fund; rather, he did not want his name to appear publicly on a list of contributors. Finally, Wolfe made some brief remarks about his distinction between patriotism and duty.[33]

Wilson began his questioning of Wolfe by asking if Wolfe felt it his duty "to conceal the fact" that he had given to the war effort by purchasing Liberty bonds and by donating to the Red Cross. Wolfe responded that he was not trying to conceal anything; it was just his "habit" not to use his name in that way. Wilson then asked, "What is the origin of that habit?" Wolfe, in his best psychological jargon, replied, "Uninterrupted action along the same line."

Wilson next moved to questions of patriotism. Wolfe espoused a philosophy of internationalism, arguing that one's duty to humankind normally came before one's duty to country. Pressed on the issue, he admitted that patriotism was justified in times of war but that in times of peace, patriotism could prove destructive. He stated, "Germany's intense patriotism . . . had more to do with the present war than any other cause."

To other questions, Wolfe responded that he had not favored America's involvement in the war but that he had come to believe that the war declaration was, in retrospect, the right decision. He noted that he was not much given to displays of emblems, although he may have worn a Red Cross button on occasion. When asked if he displayed the American flag, he replied that he had several at home and that he displayed them on appropriate holidays. Other questions were asked about the April 2 peace petition. Wolfe indicated that he had not written it but that he had been one of the early signers.

Wilson returned once again to the patriotism question.

Q. Your own notion theoretically is that as mankind progresses the natural love of country decreases?

A. I did not say that quite, I said the necessity for the love of country decreases.

Q. What is your notion as to the increase or decrease of a man's patriotism as he becomes more civilized and better educated and broader in learning?

A. That is dependent wholly upon the condition of the country; upon the need for patriotism, just the same as money or pears or any other commodity. . . . when it is needed then it is of more value than when it is not needed.

Wolfe was questioned by several members of the board, including Brown. At the conclusion of the questioning, Wilson asked him if he wished to call any witnesses on his behalf, to which Wolfe responded, "No."

Reporting on Wolfe's testimony on his subscriptions to war bonds and the Red Cross, the *Lincoln Daily Star* wrote, "The committee found . . . that Dr. Wolfe had subscribed to the different activities in proportion to his means and if anything beyond his quota." Because no amounts were mentioned in the testimony transcript from the hearings, it is difficult to know the basis for the newspaper's claim. Given the *Star*'s oft-stated pleas to rid the university of its "patriotic idlers," the newspaper's reporting on Wolfe and his testimony was reasonably favorable to him.[34]

Like the others, Wolfe was left to ponder his fate. As the hearings continued, day after day, the entire campus remained under this ominous cloud, which threatened not only Wolfe but also so many of his friends: coworkers, like Luckey, and colleagues, like Caldwell, who shared his less-militaristic views and his beliefs in individual choice. The hearings went on for two weeks, with testimony occurring on nine days, seven to nine hours each day.

On June 1, charges were dropped against two of the original eleven.[35] Luckey was called again for two more days of testimony, and the evidence against him, in the form of inflammatory statements he had made, seemed most damaging. At the request of the board, Chancellor Avery returned from Washington to testify on June 2. He was asked to comment on each of the accused and the charges against them. Avery expressed doubts about Persinger and found fault with what he called Luckey's "attitude." His only recorded comment about Wolfe was that he had heard that Wolfe had given much time to the United States Army's psychological testing efforts.[36]

In the days that followed, new names were added to the ranks of the accused. A professor of physics was called for questioning when his name was given to the board by a local citizen who had overheard him defending the professors and attacking Metcalfe. Professor Addison E. Sheldon of the history department and Professor Edgar L. Hinman, Wolfe's longtime colleague in the philosophy department, were also called to answer charges against them. After their testimony, both cases were dismissed when it was concluded that the evidence did not warrant further consideration of either man.

In the final days of the hearings, Luckey was called for testimony on two more occasions, and Persinger, who had already testified on two previous occasions, was called once more. A total of eighteen faculty members were charged in the hearings. By June 9, case dismissals had reduced that number to nine. Of that nine, two had not been on the council's original list: Wolfe and Louis Bryant Tuckerman, the professor of physics.

During the course of the hearings, the attorneys, representing the board and the council, announced a rather significant procedural change that they claimed was not really a change at all: they altered the wording of the charges against the accused. They felt it might be difficult to prove "disloyalty," the charge that Wilson had specified in his list of eight points given to the board prior to the start of the hearings. Thus, the charge was changed to "hesitating, halting, and negative support of the government."[37]

In fact, words to that effect had been part of the record from the beginning. The board of regents had first used them in its letter to the council on April 25, arguing that some faculty members might be "negative, halting, or hesitant in support of the government" but that such actions or beliefs did not necessarily constitute disloyalty. In its May 20 reply to the board, the council had said: "It is not necessary that a person be proved guilty of treason or sedition to show him to be unfit as an instructor. The fact, as you so aptly suggest in your letter of April 25, 1918, that he is 'negative, halting or hesitating in support of the government' disqualifies him." The chair of the regents, Brown, made a similar distinction in his opening remarks at the hearings. "We want information not only on disloyalty, but on halting or hesitating support of the government's war policy."[38]

When the testimony was concluded on June 11, F. M. Hall, the attorney working for the State Council of Defense, reminded the board, "The accused professors were not charged with disloyalty but . . . the charge was that they were hesitating, halting, negative and lukewarm in their support of the government." An Omaha attorney, William Gurley, made the closing arguments for the hearings. Gurley was part of Wilson's team and had questioned Wolfe on what he had said to his students about the war. Gurley recited the evidence against each of the nine professors whose cases remained.

> We have Professor Wolfe who says I subscribed to Liberty bonds but not because of patriotism but because of sense of duty. He claims patriotism carries the people off their feet. This is the statement of Professor Wolfe, an instructor of American youth. How can he be allowed to remain on the faculty? No patriotism is necessary in time of peace. How absurd that statement is. He has no emotions or enthusiasm. It's all intellectual with him.[39]

When he was finished, Gurley called for the dismissal of eight of the nine faculty members, showing hesitancy only in the case of Paul Grummann, a professor of German and fine arts. The regents announced that their decisions might not be made for several days.[40]

The decisions, in fact, were announced a week later on June 18. The board of regents exonerated six of the professors but demanded the resignations of Luckey, Persinger, and Erwin Hopt, a professor of agronomy. In addition, the board expressed its displeasure with the role played by Professors Fling and England in the hearings. Much of the "evidence" they had supplied against their colleagues did not hold up under the scrutiny of the hearings. The two were branded troublemakers by the board and told to prepare an adequate explanation of their behavior or face termination. Their explanations were later accepted by the board, and both remained on the faculty.[41]

It is believed that Luckey, Persinger, and Hopt were notified before the official announcement. Luckey received the verdict during one of his classes when a secretary interrupted to hand him a note.[42] He resigned four days later, as did Persinger and Hopt. All of the nine were contacted by the newspapers for comment shortly after the regents' decisions were announced. Only Persinger had any comment, saying he bore the regents no ill will for their decision.[43]

Reaction to the decisions was mixed. Some editorials applauded the university's action, although others called it a whitewash. The hearings received national coverage as well, from the *Sacramento Bee* to the *New York Times*, plus several journal and magazine articles. Two especially critical articles appeared in 1918, one in the *Nation* and the other in *Educational Review*. The identities of the authors are unknown, since both articles were signed with Latin pseudonyms. Both lamented the loss of academic freedom in the case and the fact that an institution of higher learning would allow itself to be bullied into a trial when the charges seemed to lack any real substance.[44]

The hearings represent the darkest moment in the history of the University of Nebraska. No other incident has involved the campus in the kind of hatred, suspicion, and anguish that dominated campus life in the spring and summer of 1918. Blame for its occurrence can be cast in a number of directions. It is possible that Governor Neville was using the trial for political gain; he announced his candidacy for reelection on June 7, toward the end of the hearings.[45] Metcalfe had clear political ambitions, if not for himself then certainly for those he supported. He used the hearings, as he did his newspaper, to promote his image of Americanism. Of course other newspapers in the state fueled the fires as well, and their editorials played a significant role in stirring up public antagonism toward the university.

Supporters of the dismissed professors blamed Chancellor Avery. They felt that Avery had been afraid of his own vulnerability to charges of being pro-German (recall his statements at the German-American rally in 1910) and that his fear had prevented him from adequately defending his faculty. Had he been willing to oppose the council more vigorously, and he clearly felt the evidence was flimsy, he might have forestalled any hearing. Finally, when he appeared on the witness stand, his testimony was not especially helpful to any of the accused, and was damaging to some.[46]

Although personal ambitions and foibles clearly contributed to the initiation and conduct of the hearings, the support of the trial may be more broadly attributed. The situation at the University of Nebraska was not unique, although one author has referred to it as "a unique, indeed, an heroic experiment in college government."[47] The same wartime hysteria and superpatriotism that motivated the Nebraska hearings existed in other states as well. The result was great misery for a number of citizens in all walks of life. People were jailed, jobs were lost, houses and businesses were burned, and families were broken up, frequently for the most trivial "crimes" of free speech. Some punishments for disloyalty were aimed at public humiliation, ranging from being tarred and feathered or covered in yellow paint, to being made to kiss the American flag.[48] Clearly the ugliness was not confined to colleges and universities; however, it seemed especially pernicious there because of the sacred canon of academic freedom.

As noted by the historian Carol Gruber, "Academic freedom was a precarious ideal in the best of times." And American involvement in World War I provided the worst of times. The fledgling American Association of University Professors (AAUP) found itself tested early, when the war began. Sadly, the organization backed away from its insistence on absolute academic freedom, arguing that this war, as a threat to the very survival of democracy, necessitated the rescinding of free speech on campus. On December 24, 1917, the AAUP's Committee on Academic Freedom and Academic Tenure released its report on academic freedom, describing four grounds for faculty dismissal. "Improper" attitudes, communicated even unintentionally, which might cause someone else (i.e., a student) to not support the war effort constituted appropriate cause for dismissal. The AAUP admitted that because of the professoriat's potential influence on the public, given the perceived authority of the university, faculty members should be rightly held to special restrictions on their speech. Commenting on the AAUP report, Gruber wrote, "Short of proscribing people's thoughts, it is hard to imagine any further possible violation of civil liberty."[49]

In Nebraska, the aftermath of the hearings was long-lasting. There were residual hard feelings within the faculty and between the faculty and administration. In the eyes of Nebraskans, the university had been damaged—damned because it found disloyalty in the faculty ranks and damned because it failed to both recognize the pervasiveness of that disloyalty and to deal with it forcefully. Unfortunately, not only did the end of the war not bring an end to the accusations, but it produced a new target—the Red, or its milder version, the Pinko.

For Wolfe, the aftermath of the ordeal of the trial was very brief, albeit consequential. The spring semester had been a tense one because of the controversy over faculty disloyalty. He had been incredibly distraught throughout the period of the hearings, fearing for his own job and those of close colleagues. His performance as a teacher had been attacked in public. His value as a faculty member had been seriously questioned. And there were those who still believed he should be dismissed. It was difficult to bear, especially for someone who had devoted all of his adult life to the improvement of education and who valued students as he did.

On July 24, five weeks after the regents had announced their decisions, Wolfe, his wife, and two of their children, Katharine and Harry, drove to Wheatland, Wyoming, to visit Wolfe's brother Vance. Wolfe looked forward to getting away from Lincoln for a while and to enjoying the relaxed atmosphere of his brother's farm. The drive had been a pleasant one, something of a new experience for him because he had made almost no long trips by car.

The Wolfe brothers were close to one another, often playing tricks on each other. Vance was especially noted for his practical jokes, and anyone could be a target, including sisters-in-law. After dinner on the evening of the Wolfes' arrival, Katharine Wolfe got up to clear the table. But Vance stopped her, saying he would take care of everything. He walked to the door, opened it, and called to his dogs, who rushed into the house and up to the table, where they licked the food off all the plates. Katharine was horrified at first but laughed later when sne learned that Vance had trained the dogs to perform for her benefit. The memory of that incident, seeing her husband and his brothers laughing together, would become bittersweet for Katharine Wolfe because of events that soon followed.

On July 30 Wolfe and his wife were working in a field when he began to complain of chest pains. Katharine took him to a nearby tent so that he could lie down. Harry, Jr., recalled looking through a slit in the tent and seeing his mother leaning over his father, crying and saying over and over, "He'll be better in a minute." But in a few hours Wolfe was dead, apparently of a heart attack, at the age of fifty-nine.

The family rode the train back to Lincoln, arriving on August 1. The funeral service was held the following day at the Wolfes' home on J Street and had to be moved outside because of the size of the crowd. Members of the university community were well represented, including Luckey and Laurence Fossler, who served as pallbearers.[50] Later that day there was a very brief ceremony at Wyuka Cemetery.

Wolfe's death was not expected by those who knew him. He had not complained of any heart problems, and to his family and friends he seemed in good health; however, in February 1918 he had written to a former student to decline an invitation to deliver a commencement address, citing his busy schedule and his health, which was "not as robust" as it had "formerly seemed to be."[51] Some friends felt that the strain of the long car trip had been too much for Wolfe; others speculated that he had overexerted himself in the field. And, of course, some argued that his death was the result of the strain of the hearings. Two items in the Lincoln newspapers put into words what other friends must have thought.

It is a shame to Nebraska that Dr. Wolfe, for no reason whatever, was dragged into the state university inquisition last June and bawled out by cheap political aspirants for public favor, trying to emphasize and capitalize their own patriotism at the expense of the reputation of better men and worthier citizens. . . . [The hearings] hurt him cruelly, and proved no doubt a contributing cause to his untimely death.

And another writer observed, "For Nebraska it was a tragedy that in the last months of a life poured out for his country this man should have had to suffer the injustice and ignominy of public questionings of his loyalty to his country."[52]

The conditions generating the hearings had been much in Wolfe's mind in the last days of his life. In the final article from his pen, an article published in the month of his death, he discussed the role of education in the creation of the *individual*. Addressing the issue of obedience, Wolfe wrote:

Society should now be strong enough to do justice to the individual and not seek to crucify or to dwarf him, hiding behind the palladium of "the king can do no wrong." There is no institution in society worth preserving that cannot withstand all attacks of individual iconoclasts. . . . Now, in truth, obedience is not a virtue any more than eating is a virtue. . . . Too much obedience may ruin character, may dwarf the intellect, may paralyse the will of children and of adults. Unquestioning reverence for authority is necessary on the frontier and in the nursery; but its overcultivation has blinded us to the greatest evils of recent days. It whips into line the doubting Thomases of all political parties. It smothers the indignation of a community when the grossest outrage is committed by its chosen officers. It immolates the individual upon a fetish long since outgrown. It is the cry which the strong have always raised to cow the weak.[53]

Many of Wolfe's friends and former students expressed anger about the events of the last months of his life, blaming the university for not protecting itself and its faculty from the paranoia and self-righteousness of people whom Samuel Johnson would have labeled "scoundrels," people seeking their last refuge in patriotism. Katharine Wolfe blamed the university for her husband's death; however, she also blamed herself. She had been active in the pacifist movement in Lincoln and had even marched in several of the peace parades. On occasion, Wolfe had defended her activities to colleagues, and perhaps students, who had questioned or disparaged pacifism. Although Katharine had never been mentioned in the hearings when Wolfe was questioned, she felt that her activities had added to suspicions about him, and she also believed that they had added to his mental strain, ultimately contributing to his death. She lived with that guilt for the rest of her life.

Katharine remained in Lincoln with her two younger children for several more years. She took a job with the Lincoln Public Schools as a school physician, inaugurating prevention strategies to minimize health problems in children. In 1925, after years of battling Lincoln physicians who opposed her promotion of hygiene courses in the schools, she moved her family to Seattle. For her, too many of the Nebraska memories were painful ones.[54]

On Wolfe's death, the headship in the Department of Philosophy passed to Hartley Burr Alexander. He had testified in the trial as a witness in support of Grummann and Caldwell.[55] Alexander had been a strong supporter of Wolfe's and wrote several moving tributes to his former professor and colleague, including Wolfe's obituary in *Science*.[56]

In a letter to the *Nation* written a week after the verdicts of the hearings were announced, Alexander argued that the hearings had signaled the evolution of a new kind of professor and a new definition for academic responsibility. He noted that during the testimony, one professor had been asked, "Have you ever at any time in your classes presented your country's cause for being in war?" The professor had answered: "Never. I teach mathematics." According to Alexander, the hearings had shown that it was the duty of professors "to voice [in class] sentiments felt by the public"; the public had the right to expect that kind of responsible citizenship from the faculties of its universities.[57]

It seems unlikely that Wolfe would have shared his former student's beliefs about mandatory politics in the classroom, and Wolfe did not live long enough to see Alexander's assessment proved wrong. The hearings were tragic enough in their own right; for them to have given birth to the legacy expressed by Alexander would have compounded the tragedy of those whose "crimes" of free speech cost them their jobs, and perhaps their lives.

Chapter Seven

A Teacher
Is Forever

In the grand scheme of events, Wolfe's death in the summer of 1918 was all but lost among the never-ending memorials. Every day, Americans were dying by the hundreds from the influenza epidemic, which reached its peak in the fall of 1918, an epidemic that would claim a half million American lives by 1919. And thousands of Americans were dying abroad in the "Great War," many of them Nebraska youth, undoubtedly some of whom had been among Wolfe's students.

There was some concern among Wolfe's friends that a memorial service for him might not be held on the university campus because of the aftermath of the hearings. Although Wolfe had been acquitted, his views on patriotism had been widely quoted in the press, and typically he had been disparaged for "spouting his treasonous philosophies while brave Americans gave their lives in foreign lands." An editorial in the *Omaha World Herald*, a paper more sympathetic to Wolfe than was the *Bee*, Omaha's Republican newspaper, called for an official tribute to his years of service at the university. "The universities are full of professors but those of the Wolfe type are very few. A half dozen such men would make any university great. . . . The university in which he was a tower of strength should not allow his passing to go unnoticed."[1]

The memorial service for Wolfe, held at Memorial Hall in December 1918, a month after the armistice, gave many Nebraskans a chance to remember their former colleague, teacher, and friend. The chair of the regents, E. P. Brown, gave a brief talk about the role of the scholar-teacher, with Wolfe as an exemplar. The most moving part of the service was a collection of former students's tributes prepared by Ned C. Abbott, a graduate of the pedagogy program and the head of the Nebraska School for the Blind in Nebraska City. At the time of the memorial service, Abbott was ill with flu, and Winifred Hyde read the tributes he had prepared.

Some of Wolfe's faculty colleagues began in 1918 to work toward a more lasting memorial. Laurence Fossler, a boyhood friend of Wolfe's and a professor of German at the university,[2] Thomas F. A. Williams, an attorney and one of Wolfe's former students, and Howard Caldwell sought to raise money for a fellowship in Wolfe's name. They pursued their fund drive through the Palladian Society, the first literary society founded at the university in 1871. Fossler, Caldwell, and Wolfe had all been Palladians together as undergraduates. The decision was made to establish the fellowship for graduate study in psychology or philosophy. At the time, the university had no funds for graduate fellowships, and the state had made it clear that appropriated money could not be used for that purpose.

The Palladians hoped to use the Wolfe fellowship as a model of privately endowed fellowships that would allow Nebraska's finest students to continue their studies at home and that would draw talent from other states into Nebraska for graduate work. The Palladians set an ambitious goal of ten thousand dollars for the endowment, three thousand dollars of which was to come from members of the literary society. Their campaign was communicated to former students in several announcements published and mailed during 1919–20.[3] The smaller sum was collected by 1920 and turned over to the university. Other sums were added, and finally in 1925 the accumulated interest was sufficient to fund the first student, W. H. Werkmeister. Donations continued to arrive, so that the ten-thousand-dollar goal was achieved in 1930.[4] The Wolfe memorial fellowship marked the first such private endowment for graduate study at the university.

The consequences of Wolfe's involvement in the 1918 hearings are nowhere more evident than in the opening of the Social Sciences Hall in 1920, a building that housed the new psychology laboratories that Wolfe had planned in the last year of his life. Thus the object of Wolfe's struggles for thirty years was finally a reality. For his friends, it seemed fitting that the labs be named in honor of him: the H. K. Wolfe Memorial Psychology Laboratory. Hartley Alexander, as the chair of the Department of Philosophy, supported such a plan. However, it was not to be. No written record exists to indicate why the plan failed, or even if the naming of the laboratory was ever made as a formal proposal to the administration. Perhaps the administration and regents felt that naming the labs in honor of Wolfe would resurrect the memories of the disloyalty hearings, drawing the ire of those critics who considered the judgments a whitewash. It is understandable that many in the university community, including some of Wolfe's friends, would have wanted those issues laid to rest. Although the psychology laboratory did not bear Wolfe's name, it did bear his stamp, and for a while at least, there were those who remembered his role in establishing the "new" psychology in Nebraska.

The psychology laboratory was a part of Wolfe's legacy. Yet its value was not defined in terms of his research. Some of his psychophysical studies—for example, those on the estimation of the middle of lines—received attention in the 1940s when the field of human-factors psychology was working on problems associated with human operators reading signals from radar screens.[5] However, in contemporary psychology, his research is all but forgotten.

Similarly, the child study work, although of historical interest, is not cited in the contemporary literature of psychology. Instead, the value of Wolfe's work was that it focused attention on the needs of Nebraska's schoolchildren, emphasizing the significance of individual differences for educational planning and the importance of psychology for teacher training. Although his work had some influence on education within the state, it had no discernible effect on the advancement of the fields of educational and developmental psychology.

Instead, Wolfe's laboratory proved to be an important recruiting mechanism, drawing many young people into the science of psychology. At their age, he had believed in the old psychology, arguing in his senior commencement address that the nature of the soul would be revealed by a rational analysis of its manifestations. However, converted by his experiences in Germany, he offered his students the chance to unlock the secrets of the mind by an experimental analysis of the products of consciousness.

Wolfe did not found his laboratory for purposes of student recruitment; he simply knew no way to teach the science of psychology without "some things to see and feel."[6] One of Wolfe's students, Madison Bentley, who graduated in 1895 and later became an eminent professor of psychology, recalled in his autobiography the influence of the laboratory work.

> During the teaching years I have often tried to recover the best things in my own early instruction that I might use them for inspiring junior [undergraduate] students. . . . Interesting exercises in the primitive but resourceful laboratory which I first entered accompanied the lectures and discussions of the initial course. The exercises were impressive and they formed associative nodes. But it was, as I now recover the course, the dissection at first-hand of the sheep's brain which seemed most definitely to put me sympathetically inside psychology. That I was then acquiring sound and relevant knowledge, and not being merely entertained, I have had frequent occasion to realize. And so far from inclining toward a mere anatomy of the brain, those simple but absorbing dissections seem now to have done more than anything else has to form a working conception of the organism which is strictly psychology. . . . That early teacher—to revert to primary influences—was a very engaging man. It may well be that the experiments and dissection were impressive and instructive mainly because they were the modes of Wolfe's teaching.[7]

Clearly the laboratory did for Bentley what Wolfe intended it to do—get him "inside psychology."

Wolfe's laboratory was an avenue for demonstrating the phenomena and principles of psychology; however, its greater purpose was to get students involved in research. And as he wrote, "[Research] is the sole method of growth." It was by research that the infant in the cradle learned about the world. And it was no different for adults. Mental growth came from questioning, working through complex problems, and self-initiated exploring. Recall that Wolfe believed those activities had been largely eliminated when children submitted too fully to the authority of the schools. It was the job of the university teacher to restore those primitive intellectual activities, training students to educate themselves in the life that followed formal education.[8]

As an educator, Wolfe was an unqualified success. His popularity as a professor was evidenced in part by the growth of his psychology programs. In his initial year at the university he had 21 students in his psychology classes. When he was dismissed in 1897, that number had increased to 225, a tenfold increase in a university that underwent a fourfold increase in enrollment during the same period. Those enrollments are especially impressive when one considers that students did not receive credit for the laboratory hours that were part of the course in general psychology. Thus they enrolled in Wolfe's classes knowing they faced greater time requirements than would be demanded for other classes of comparable credit hours. There were extra time demands outside of lecture and lab hours as well; Wolfe's reputation was that of an instructor who assigned considerable reading and writing. As Alexander described him in his remarks at Wolfe's funeral, "[His classes were] notoriously difficult; there was no room for the slacker there; but there never was an uninteresting lecture hour, and year after year the students filed in, willing to venture the work for the sake of the zest."[9]

Consistent with his views on mental growth, Wolfe continually prodded his students to think. They were taught to question "givens" and to recognize the fallibility of authoritative sources. It was not acceptable to say that habit was such and such because William James said so. Students were encouraged to work through problems and issues on their own. He

Wolfe with his wife, Katharine, and their two younger children, Katharine and Harry, in front of their home on J Street (June 1918)

had a knack, according to some of his students, for leading students to the path of intellectual discovery and then making them proceed on their own. He believed that knowledge gained by self-discovery held more meaning and, most important, that it strengthened one's intellectual abilities. As a part of this process, students were encouraged to disagree with him, and he rewarded such disagreements when they were evidently based on sound reasoning and appropriate investigation. In contemporary educational jargon, Wolfe's emphasis might be described as critical thinking. Indeed, some of his teaching methods correspond to steps common to current models.

Allied to Wolfe's demand that students think was his insistence that they have courage for their views. He did not encourage dogmatism, nor could he abide faintheartedness or wavering. If their scholarship was sound, students should have confidence in their conclusions and be willing to defend them against alternative views. Taking a stand on questions was a moral duty inherent in scholarship.

One of Wolfe's own stands angered at least one of his students. Apparently he was not immune to the dogma of his day, despite his admonitions to students about accepting statements at face value. Alvin Johnson, a student at the University of Nebraska in the 1890s and later the president of the New School for Social Research in New York City, was in a quandary as a young man, trying to decide if he should switch his course of study from the classics to the social sciences. Johnson asked his friend Hartley Alexander to ask Wolfe for advice. Wolfe, observing that Johnson was proficient in languages, a skill suggesting good memory abilities, told him to stay in the classics. Wolfe argued that social sciences required reasoning powers and that memory and reason typically did not go together as traits. Johnson described his reaction to Wolfe's advice in his autobiography.

> If I still had doubts they disappeared with the message from Wolfe. I had never thought much of him as a psychologist. He had worked with Wundt and was bent on fobbing off the student's natural curiosity about the workings of the mind with huge doses of the physiology of the brain and the nervous system. It was like him, I thought, to cling to the exploded notion of the incompatibility of reason and memory. I was angry, and anger is a helpful factor in resolution.[10]

Teachers never please everyone, and Wolfe was no exception. Likely he would have welcomed Johnson's disagreement, seeing in him an embracing of the same rational psychology that Wolfe had espoused at a similar age.[11]

Just as he demanded much of his students, Wolfe demanded much of himself. Preparation for his lectures and laboratories involved careful planning and continual refinement. He did not allow his notes to yellow. One of Wolfe's laboratory assistants wrote: "His outlines were made over fresh every year. . . . His laboratory work was changed as well. Students who perfected themselves on the tests in sensation and memory from notes or outlines of a previous class, learned when they reached the laboratory, that there was an entirely new set of experiments."[12] Perhaps only teachers can understand the commitment required by such a practice.

Wolfe argued that the lecture was not an effective tool for learning, yet he was a masterful lecturer, typically using it to prod his students into thinking about and reacting to his comments. One of his students recalled: "His lectures were never over in fifty minutes. Usually they went buzzing around in the student's brain for weeks afterward. . . . Not infrequently the whole class poured forth from the lecture room 'hopping mad,' as they expressed it, because he had turned loose a flood of raillery at certain of their pet hobbies."[13]

Virtually every description of Wolfe as a lecturer by his former students includes the word *inspiring*. His inspiration came from his personal qualities as a lecturer—organization, explanatory skills, humor (sometimes sarcastic in nature), optimism, and humility. Partly his inspiration came from his vision for psychology. He preached to his students the refrain that psychology held great promise for solving the problems of the world. He believed that some knowledge of the discipline would be helpful to any student, regardless of the student's chosen field.

Wolfe's ability to inspire also came from the breadth of his knowledge. He was extremely well read in a number of diverse fields, and he brought that breadth to bear on his lectures with frequent references from such subjects as art, literature, history, archeology, and biology. His addiction to books was well known; he liked to read them and was constantly buying them. He would bring home a wonderful new set of Shakespeare's plays, only to have his family point out that he already had three others.

Wolfe used his ability to inspire to sway his students. Before hiring Edgar Hinman, he had questioned Pillsbury, "Will he help my department's *influence* over students?" Wolfe meant to influence his students because he believed so strongly in the value of what he was teaching.[14] He sought converts to the new psychology, and evidence of his incredible success is presented in the Appendix. His imprinting was strong, and many of his students credited more influence to him than to their doctoral advisors. Two of his three students who became president of the American Psychological Association, Madison Bentley and Edwin Guthrie, labeled Wolfe their greatest influence, even though they took their doctoral degrees with such eminent figures as Edward Bradford Titchener and Edgar Arthur Singer. Walter Pillsbury, the third of the APA presidents, listed both Wolfe and Titchener (his doctoral mentor) as his greatest influences.[15]

Hinman has written that Wolfe's genius for teaching was partly the result of his passion for human welfare. His lectures gave most of his courses an applied bent, a characteristic that added to their appeal to students. In the lecture and the laboratory there were frequent examples illustrating the utility of the principles or the existence of the phenomena of psychology outside the university. For Wolfe, an appreciation of applicability was important in stimulating lifelong learning.[16]

Wolfe's passion for human welfare embodied his concern for ethics. Part of what he discussed with his students was "right behavior and right thinking." Indeed, *ethical* was the companion descriptor to *inspiring* in the letters written about Wolfe. Rufus Bentley, Alexander, Abbott, and Hinman are among his students and colleagues who have written about Wolfe's teaching of ethics—how he made ethics a part of his courses and how he modeled ethical values in his own behavior. Wolfe's papers contain more than twenty lectures associated with the topic of ethics. He told his students that ethics implied action—conduct. It was not enough to *be* right, one had to *do* right. Further, right conduct was constant; it did not "vary with the winds of public opinion."[17] For Wolfe, right conduct meant making the world a better place. It was not right, for example, to be content that the condition of the working class was better than it had been. He asked his students, "[Is it] not possible to abolish *poverty* as slavery has been abolished?"[18] He championed the applicability of psychology to solving the problems of the world, and his lifelong commitment to improving educational practices represented his efforts in that regard.

Wolfe's view of ethics was bound up in a consciousness that recognized the "unity of the world." Wolfe explained: "[This concept] is the end of all philosophy of all Ethics and of all religion. This may be what Socrates meant by insisting on the impossibility of wrong action except through ignorance. This is the secret and often mystic source of the many cries of humanity for closer relationships. The brotherhood of man has no meaning apart from such a conception."[19] Of course, this world view is recognizably one of the causes of the difficulties Wolfe faced in the 1918 hearings.

Over the course of his life, Wolfe modified his views of human conduct. According to his daughter Isabel: "He softened somewhat his rigid rules for right conduct. He realized that the human race is subject to forces as yet beyond the control of humanity. Thus, in a way, he endured the tide of war-hysteria realizing that man can be his own worst enemy, and that the struggle will be prolonged far beyond his early hopes."[20]

As Wolfe cared about humanity in a global sense, he cared deeply for his own students. There was never a doubt that most of his energies went toward their benefit. He was a selfless man whose satisfaction was derived from the accomplishments of his students. Students of all intellectual stripes found him to be a willing mentor; he was interested in them whether they were headed for graduate work or for work in Nebraska's kindergartens. Students were frequent dinner guests in the Wolfes' home. Indeed, Isabel recalled that in her youth there were few dinners that did not involve one or more of her father's students at the table. Wolfe loaned students money, often put them up at his house when they were in need, and worked to get them jobs.

Wolfe's caring for his students, his philosophy of education, and his personal ethic made him a very demanding educator when it came to his dealings with the university's administrators or with school-board members. He was not able to accept "no" for an answer when he believed his request was justified, and of course that caused him serious problems on more than one occasion. Pearse, the former superintendent of the Omaha public schools, commented on this difficulty of Wolfe's when he described Wolfe as lacking diplomacy. Bessey, the former chancellor of the university, noted Wolfe's "strong convictions that were frankly expressed."[21] Howard Caldwell, Wolfe's classmate from the Class of 1880 and a faculty member in Nebraska's Department of History, painted a similar picture of his former colleague in a letter of recommendation he wrote when Wolfe was leaving the public schools of South Omaha in 1901.

> He is honorable, high-minded, and courageous. He is frank, perhaps to a fault, never descending to duplicity and double-dealing. When a wrong is clearly seen, he has the manhood to try to right it, even if it may be an unpopular act; yet Dr. Wolfe is not seeking for errors; he is an open, cheerful, companionable man. He is a large man in every sense of the word, physically, mentally, and morally.[22]

Those traits that most people saw as courage and honesty, others viewed as self-righteousness and an inability to compromise. Traits that led most of his students to see him as a paragon led some, perhaps many, of his employers to see him as arrogant. Wolfe was neither, and yet some of both. The former is in greater evidence, yet there are occasional glimpses of the latter. For example, in a letter to Pillsbury in 1897, shortly after being fired, Wolfe wrote, "Of course no new man can get the students I would have had." Indeed, he "got" students, hundreds of them, and as one described it, he infected them for life.[23]

Wolfe will continue to occupy little more than a footnote in the American psychology histories to be written. His name will occasionally be listed among those American students who studied with Wundt. And when listings of the early psychology laboratories are published, his name will appear there as well. Yet he will not be found in the subject indexes of these histories. He made no research discoveries of lasting significance, he founded no journals nor did he serve as principal editor of one, he generated no original theories, and he developed no psychological tests. There are no eponyms for Wolfe—no Wolfe maze, no Wolfe chronoscope, no Wolfe test of social maturity, no Wolfian psychology, not even a Wolfian hypothesis.

It should be clear that Wolfe did not set out to be an eponym. He did not choose to play his role on a national stage. The personal ambition and entrepreneurial talents that were so evident in G. Stanley Hall and James McKeen Cattell were absent in Wolfe.[24] Instead, he chose to spend his career as a teacher in the West, as he called it. At several points in his career, there were employment offers that would have taken him away from Nebraska, yet with the exception of his one-year sojourn to Montana, he stayed in his adopted home state after 1889.

Wolfe's decision to reside in Nebraska is certainly related to his obscurity. American psychology was happening largely in the East, at universities such as Columbia, Cornell, Clark, Johns Hopkins, and Harvard. There were early psychology laboratories in the Midwest, such as the ones at universities in Indiana, Wisconsin, and Iowa, as well as Nebraska, yet despite their establishment by well-trained psychologists, these labs never achieved the prestige of those in the East. Psychology faculties there were larger, libraries better funded, and laboratories better equipped. Further, the focus of eastern training in the new psychology was on graduate students. Thus the first generation of homegrown American psychology doctorates came mostly from the East.

Midwestern psychologists had a difficult time being part of organized psychology. The American Psychological Association was ten years old when it held its annual meeting in 1901 in a city that many of its members likely considered the westernmost edge of American civilization—Chicago. Prior to that time the association had met no farther west than Philadelphia. Thus the midwesterners had to travel east each year for the annual meetings, which were held during the Christmas holidays. The leaders of the other principal midwestern laboratories, Joseph Jastrow of the University of Wisconsin, William Lowe Bryan of Indiana University, and Carl E. Seashore of the University of Iowa, actively participated in the annual meetings of the APA, and all three were elected to the presidency of the association between 1900 and 1911.

Although Wolfe was a charter member of the APA, he allowed his membership to lapse. According to one of his letters, he rejoined in 1916 when he attended the annual meeting that year in New York City.[25] It is not known if he attended any of the APA meetings prior to that one; probably he did not. Interestingly, there is no evidence that he attended any of the four meetings held in Philadelphia between 1892 and 1914, which he could have combined with a family visit to Katharine's relatives there. Perhaps his absence was due to the expenses associated with attending the meetings, or it may have been due to a reluctance to leave his family during the Christmas season. His letters suggest both as possibilities. However, another interpretation is that organized psychology held little interest for him. The principal advantage, perhaps the only one, for his attendance at the APA meetings would have been to make personal contacts with other psychologists to better assist his students in getting fellowships for graduate study. And yet he was already succeeding well in that endeavor, placing students at Cornell, Columbia, Clark, and Chicago. Titchener, in particular, welcomed Wolfe's students because they were so well trained in experimental methods.

In short, Wolfe chose to spend his life as a teacher of psychology and he chose to do it in Nebraska. *Chose* may, in fact, be the wrong word because *choice* implies a consideration of alternatives and there is no evidence that Wolfe ever considered being anything other than a teacher. His sense of self was wrapped up in what he was able to accomplish with his students. To have the kind of influence that he enjoyed required that he set aside ambitions for personal accomplishment. It also required a host of personal qualities that define only the best of educators, as indicated in his obituary published in *Science*. "There are few qualities which the teacher should possess which he did not own in exalted measure. Keenness, kindness, unfailing humor and patience and generosity of soul, and the power to inspire, all these were his; and he was loved by those under his influence as few men are loved."[26]

The American historian Henry Brooks Adams has written, "A teacher affects eternity; he can never tell where his influence will stop."[27] And such is Wolfe's legacy, continued through generations of his students and their students and their students and beyond. It is an invisible legacy but no less important than the legacies of his better-known contemporaries. Wolfe's immortality resides in the thousands who bear his imprint, without ever knowing his name.

Appendix

Psychologists Who Studied under Harry Kirke Wolfe

Wolfe spent twenty-one and a half years as a college professor, with only one year of that outside the University of Nebraska. During that time he worked largely with undergraduate students, although he supervised some master's degree students in education after 1895 and some master's degree students in philosophy and psychology after his return to Nebraska in 1906.

Among Wolfe's students were many who became successful as attorneys, as business owners, and particularly as schoolteachers and administrators. However, this appendix will focus solely on those students who pursued careers in psychology. It will exclude students who pursued traditional philosophy as opposed to psychology, with one exception: Hartley Burr Alexander.

The twenty-two who appear in the following listing are classified as Wolfe's students based on one or more lines of evidence: acknowledgments they gave Wolfe in published sources or personal letters, letters of recommendation Wolfe wrote for them for graduate study or employment, their work as psychology laboratory assistants for Wolfe, and, in a few cases, the appearance of their names in his grade books. The last does not guarantee that Wolfe had any influence over the student, yet the few who meet only that criterion are included in this appendix in the interest of comprehensiveness. Certainly some students were more strongly influenced than others.

Hartley Burr Alexander (1873–1939)

Born in Lincoln, Nebraska, Alexander received his baccalaureate degree in 1897, the year Wolfe was fired. He earned his doctorate in 1901 at Columbia University, where he studied with James McKeen Cattell. Wolfe brought him back to the University of Nebraska in 1910 and he taught most of the philosophy classes plus a psychology course entitled "Suggestion and Psychotherapy." After Wolfe's death, Alexander served as the head of the Department of Philosophy until 1927 when he accepted a professorship at Scripps College in Claremont, California. He remained there until his death. His eminence in philosophy earned him the presidency of the American Philosophical Association in 1920. He was a diverse scholar who published in history, anthropology, and philosophy, in addition to writing poetry, plays, and operas.

Alexander was also interested in architecture. He provided the symbols and inscriptions that appear on the Nebraska Capitol. Given his testimony during the 1918 hearings at the University of Nebraska and his views on a professor's duty to reflect public sentiment, one of his inscriptions seems especially salient. It is carved above the capitol's north entrance: "The salvation of the state is watchfulness in the citizen."[1]

Alexander did similar work for other buildings, including the Los Angeles Public Library, the Fidelity Mutual Life Insurance Building in Philadelphia, Rockefeller Center in New York City, and the Century of Progress Exposition in Chicago. In 1988 he was elected the twenty-second member of the Nebraska Hall of Fame. His bust is displayed, along with those of the other honorees, in the capitol.[2]

Rose Gustava Anderson (1893–1978)

Anderson was born in Gothenburg, Nebraska, on June 23, 1893. She earned both her baccalaureate (1917) and master's degrees (1918) at the University of Nebraska and then accepted a position as a psychologist with the Minnesota State Board of Control. After four years in that position she journeyed to New York City, where she completed her doctorate at Columbia University in 1925. Returning to Minnesota, Anderson worked for the next five years as a psychologist for the Minneapolis Child Guidance Clinic. During that time she collaborated with Frederick Kuhlmann (see later listing), another of Wolfe's students, on the development of an intelligence test, the *Kuhlmann-Anderson Intelligence Test* (1927), and on a test of academic potential.

In 1930, Anderson returned to New York as the director of the Westchester County Children's Association. She held that position for twelve years, until she resigned to become vice-president of the Psychological Corporation, the major publisher of psychological tests in the United States. Her specialty was in the assessment of mentally retarded children, an area of interest that grew in importance after World War II. She retired from the corporation in 1958. Her honors included election as a fellow in the American Psychological Association and a listing in the 1974–75 edition of *Who's Who in America*.

Henry J. Arnold (1887–1959)

Born in Sterling, Nebraska, on February 11, 1887, Arnold earned his baccalaureate degree at Nebraska in 1917. He taught school in Bristow and Sterling, Nebraska, and then in Waverly, Iowa. In 1925 he joined the faculty at Wittenberg College in Springfield, Ohio, as a professor of psychology and the director of the Division of Special Schools. While there, he completed his doctoral study at Ohio State University.

Arnold's research interests were in the field of college students' performance; he published studies on student motivation, remedial methods, and subject deficiencies, especially in math and English. Those interests led him to look at college teaching methods, a field in which he also wrote. He authored one book, *Research Adventures in University Teaching* (1927).

After receiving his Ph.D. in 1929, Arnold's initial postdoctorate job was as the dean of a junior college in Dayton, Ohio, a job he held for ten years. He left Dayton in 1939 to accept the presidency of Hartwick College, a Lutheran college in Oneonta, New York, where he served until his retirement in 1954. Arnold was the first layperson to be president of Hartwick, and his tenure marked a period of economic success for the college. He established a school of nursing, funded a number of new buildings, and increased the college's endowment by more than 250 percent.[3]

Charles Homer Bean (1870–1940)

Bean was born in Petersburg, Ohio, on February 28, 1870, and completed his undergraduate degree at Nebraska in 1899 at the age of twenty-nine. After graduation he taught in public schools before joining the faculty at Indiana Normal College, a post he held from 1903 to 1914. During a leave of absence he completed his doctorate in psychology at Columbia University in 1912. He left Indiana in 1914 to become head of the Department of Philosophy and Education at Louisiana State University (LSU).

Bean's research interests were eclectic and included mental development, the course of forgetting, vocational education, the psychology of language, and job analyses of athletics. He retired from LSU in 1940 and died a few months later.

Charles Emile Benson (1881–1963)

Benson was born in Clinton, Iowa, on September 9, 1881. He earned his A.B. (1911) and A.M. (1912) degrees from Nebraska, studying with both Wolfe and Luckey and serving for two years as Wolfe's lab assistant. After two years of public school teaching in Lexington, Nebraska, Benson taught for a year at the Nebraska State Teachers College in Kearney and then served for six years as the head of the Department of Psychology at Southeast Missouri State Teachers College at Cape Girardeau.

In 1922, Benson received his Ph.D. from Columbia University. He then taught for a year at the University of Oklahoma before returning to New York as a member of the educational psychology faculty at New York University. He was named chair of that department in 1929, a post he held until 1943. Benson retired from NYU in 1945.

Much of Benson's research involved thinking processes in children and ways to improve mental efficiency. His books included *Psychology for Teachers* (1926) and *Psychology for Advertisers* (1930).[4]

Isaac Madison Bentley (1870–1955)

Madison Bentley was born in Clinton, Iowa, on June 18, 1870. He came to Nebraska when his father accepted a pastorate in Lincoln, and he enrolled in the university in 1890. He was attracted to psychology in his first course with Wolfe and followed in the footsteps of his brother (Rufus) as Wolfe's laboratory assistant in his senior year. After graduation in 1895, Bentley received a fellowship to pursue his doctorate with Titchener at Cornell University, where he finished in 1899. He remained at Cornell as an assistant professor until 1912 when he joined the faculty at the University of Illinois as a professor and the head of the Department of Psychology.

It was during his tenure at Illinois that Bentley was elected to the presidency of the American Psychological Association in 1925. His presidential address, entitled "The Major Categories of Psychology," was a critical review of the principal schools of psychology then vying for dominance; it was illustrative of the kind of critical scholarship for which Bentley was noted. Titchener called him psychology's "most able critic."

After sixteen years at Illinois, Bentley returned to Cornell in 1928, replacing Titchener as the Sage Professor of Psychology. He held that post until his retirement in 1938, after which he continued his long association as coeditor of the *American Journal of Psychology*, an editorial tenure that spanned forty-seven years. In the course of his academic career at Illinois and Cornell, Bentley supervised the doctoral dissertations of more than forty students. Among his nearly two hundred publications, his best-known works were two books (1924 and 1934) that sought a conceptual integration of the broad field of psychology. In 1935 he was awarded an honorary doctoral degree from the University of Nebraska.[5]

Frank Gilbert Bruner (1874–1965)
Born in Streator, Illinois, on March 28, 1874, Bruner never took a class from Wolfe. He was an undergraduate at Nebraska in the period when Wolfe was in the public schools of South Omaha and Lincoln. However, the two worked together in summer education programs, and when Bruner finished his baccalaureate degree in 1903, Wolfe wrote letters of recommendation for him to Cattell at Columbia.

Bruner was accepted at Columbia, where he earned a Ph.D. in psychology in 1905 and an M.D. in 1909. While a student at Columbia, Bruner was Robert S. Woodworth's assistant for the anthropometric and psychometric labs at the Louisiana Purchase Exposition in St. Louis. Like Wolfe, Bruner spent his career applying psychology to education. As the director of Special Schools for Chicago, he pioneered programs in the education of exceptional children, especially deaf children.

Margaret Wooster Curti (1891–1961)
Curti, born in Silver Creek, Nebraska, finished her undergraduate degree at Nebraska in 1913 and her doctorate at the University of Chicago in 1920. She was a faculty member at Beloit College (1920–22), Smith College (1922–37), Teachers College of Columbia University (1937–42), and the University of Wisconsin (1943–54). Her research focused on the psychological testing of normal and delinquent children. Among her publications was a popular textbook, *Child Psychology* (1930, revised in 1938).

Horace Bidwell English (1892–1961)
English was born in Eagle, Nebraska, on October 1, 1892. He spent two years at the University of Nebraska (1909–11) before a Rhodes Scholarship took him to Oxford University, where he graduated in 1914. Writing to Wolfe from Oxford, English noted of his experience, "People are right to say that a man changes over here."[6]

After receiving his doctorate in 1916 from Yale University,

English was a member of the faculties of Wellesley College (1916–21), Antioch College (1921–25, 1927–30), and Wesleyan University (1925–27) before accepting a professorship at Ohio State University in 1930. He remained there for the rest of his career.

English published more than one hundred scientific articles on a variety of topics, many of them related to educational psychology: intelligence of schoolchildren, mental deficiency, fatigue, emotion, and the reliability and validity of tests. His books include works on learning and child psychology. However, he is best remembered for his authorship of a comprehensive dictionary of psychological terms. That publication began in 1928 as a small book, *A Student's Dictionary of Psychological Terms*, and was expanded in subsequent editions into an extensive work entitled *A Comprehensive Dictionary of Psychological and Psychoanalytical Terms* (1958).

English received a number of honors in his career. He was elected president of the Midwestern Psychological Association and was elected a fellow in both the American Psychological Association and the British Psychological Society.

Cora Louisa Friedline (1893–1975)

Friedline was born on January 21, 1893, in New York City. She was often in trouble as a youngster, and so her mother sent her to live with the mother's older sister in Lincoln. In her senior year at the University of Nebraska, Friedline took a psychology course with Wolfe and "fell desperately in love with the professor."[7] She changed her major from Greek and Latin and took an entire year of psychology, finishing her A.B. degree in 1913. She stayed at the university, serving as Wolfe's laboratory assistant, and completed her master's degree in 1915 with a thesis on precocious children in the Lincoln schools.

Friedline began work on her doctorate in psychology at Bryn Mawr College in 1915 but the following year moved to Cornell, where she worked with Titchener. She received her Ph.D. there in 1918 with a dissertation on cutaneous sensitivity (using Ernst Weber's classic two-point threshold method). Like many women doctorates of her day who chose to work in the academy, she was employed by a woman's college—Randolph-Macon Woman's College in Lynchburg, Virginia—where she taught from 1918 until her retirement in 1962. Friedline wrote to Isabel Wolfe Hemenway, "The major and biggest factor in my entire life has been and is your father Dr. Harry Kirk [sic] Wolfe—*I live to be his monument!*"[8] Upon her death in 1975, she left two hundred thousand dollars to the University of Nebraska in honor of Wolfe.

Edwin Ray Guthrie (1886–1959)

Guthrie was born in Lincoln, Nebraska, on January 9, 1886. It was as a student at Lincoln High School that he first met Wolfe. They were later reunited at the University of Nebraska when Wolfe returned to the faculty there in 1906. Guthrie finished his A.B. degree that year and remained to work on a master's degree with Wolfe. He completed that degree in 1910, and his doctorate was earned in philosophy in 1912 at the University of Pennsylvania.

Guthrie taught mathematics in a Philadelphia high school for two years before accepting a faculty position in philosophy at the University of Washington in 1914. He moved into the psychology department in 1919 and remained a member of that faculty until his retirement in 1956. For eight years he served as the dean of the Graduate School.

Guthrie's scholarship contributed to a number of areas of psychology, including social psychology, abnormal psychology, and educational psychology. His 1938 book *The Psychology of Human Conflict* was an important impetus to the field of clinical psychology. However, he is best known for his contributions to learning theory, an area he began studying in the early 1920s. The publication of his book *The Psychology of Learning*, in 1935, established him as one of the key theoreticians in that area. His theory was a deceptively simple one, emphasizing the important role of contiguity in learning. Most textbooks today list Guthrie as one of four principal neobehaviorists, the others being Clark L. Hull, Edward C. Tolman, and B. F. Skinner.

Guthrie's many honors include an honorary doctorate from the University of Nebraska in 1945, the presidency of the

American Psychological Association in 1945, and the Gold Medal Award from the American Psychological Foundation in 1958. The citation for that award noted the large number of students he stimulated to pursue careers in psychology, thus extending the legacy of his Nebraska mentor.[9]

Thomas Nicholas Jenkins (1892–1962)

Born in Mapleton, Iowa, on May 2, 1892, Jenkins earned his A.B. and A.M. degrees with Wolfe in 1915 and 1916. He stayed for a year after completing his master's degree to work as Wolfe's assistant in the psychology lab. After completing a doctorate in psychology at Columbia University in 1927, he taught on the faculty of New York University from 1927 until his retirement in 1958.

Jenkins published research in a variety of areas. He wrote several articles on mathematical psychology and coauthored three books on comparative psychology with Carl J. Warden, another of Wolfe's students (see later listing). But he was best known for his work in personality and industrial psychology, including the development of the *Jenkins Global Personality Inventory*, a personality test that enjoyed some popularity for use in selection processes by businesses and colleges.[10]

Frederick Kuhlmann (1876–1941)

Kuhlmann was born on March 20, 1876, in Davenport, Iowa. Drawn into psychology by Wolfe, he finished his undergraduate study in 1899 with Albert Ross Hill, after Wolfe's firing. He stayed on at Nebraska, earning a master's degree in 1901. He received his Ph.D. in psychology in 1903 at Clark University, where he studied with G. Stanley Hall and Edmund C. Sanford (1859–1924). Kuhlmann remained at Clark as an instructor in psychology for four years, with a one-year leave as a laboratory assistant in Joseph Jastrow's department at the University of Wisconsin.

In 1907, Kuhlmann began a three-year appointment at the University of Illinois. However, his love was psychological testing, and so he left the university to become the director of research for the Minnesota School for the Feebleminded at Faribault. He remained there from 1910 through 1921, when he became the director of research for the Department of Public Institutions for the State of Minnesota. He held that position until his death in 1941.

Kuhlmann's dissertation research involved measuring mental deficiency, a topic that set the stage for his lifelong interests. His 1912 version of the Binet-Simon intelligence test was one of the earliest translations of that test. He created a later version that allowed for the testing of infants. Kuhlmann was particularly interested in memory and mental imagery, and he published many articles on those topics, believing they were primary intellectual abilities. This work culminated in 1927 with the publication of the *Kuhlmann-Anderson Intelligence Test* (see the earlier section on Rose Anderson). His *Handbook of Mental Tests* (1922) was one of the earliest works to provide a comprehensive review of the diversity of available psychological tests.[11]

William Severt Larson (1899–1976)

Larson was born in Stromsburg, Nebraska, on September 4, 1899. He completed his baccalaureate degree in 1920 with a joint major in philosophy and music. For two years he served as the director of music for the public schools of Seward, Nebraska, and then in 1922–23 as the head of the Public School Music Department of Nebraska Wesleyan University. In 1923 he began a two-year period on the music faculty of Northwest Missouri State Teachers College in Maryville.

Larson began his graduate study in 1925 at the University of Iowa, where he worked with Carl Emil Seashore (1866–1949), America's foremost authority on the psychology of music and the developer of a series of music-talent tests that were used in public schools through the 1960s. Like his Iowa mentor, Larson published works dealing with the measurement of musical talent and the structure of music education.

After completing his doctorate in 1928, Larson joined the faculty of the Eastman School of Music in Rochester, New York, as the chair of the Department of Music Education. He held that post until his retirement in 1965. (See later listing for

Hazel Martha Stanton.) Larson appeared in six consecutive editions of *American Men and Women of Science* (the seventh through the twelfth), and in the sixth edition of *Who's Who in Music*.

Bertha Musson Luckey (1890–1966)

Bertha Luckey was the daughter of Wolfe's colleague and friend George W. A. Luckey. She was born in Ontario, California, on January 2, 1890, and was thus three months younger than Isabel Wolfe. The two grew up together in Lincoln and were close friends throughout their lives.

Luckey took all of her degrees at the University of Nebraska: A.B. (1910), A.M. (1912), and Ph.D. (1916). With her degree in educational psychology, awarded through the College of Education, she was Wolfe's one doctoral student. After graduation she became the chief psychologist for the Cleveland Public Schools, a post she held until her retirement in 1957. She also held an adjunct faculty position at Cleveland's Western Reserve University. Her publications included work on personality development, measures for assessing educational progress, and methods for teaching mentally retarded children. She is best known for her research on the assessment of intelligence, particularly in mentally retarded children.

Frederick Hansen Lund (1894–1965)

Lund was born in Kairanga, New Zealand, on April 4, 1894. He studied at the University of Nebraska from 1917 to 1923, earning his A.B. degree there in 1921. His doctorate was received in 1925 from Columbia University, where he studied with the famous physiologist and psychologist, Walter B. Cannon (1871–1945). After three years at Bucknell University (1927–30), Lund joined the faculty at Temple University, where he was a professor of psychology and the head of the department until his retirement in 1959. He taught an additional five years at California State College in Los Angeles until his death in 1965.

Influenced by Cannon's views on the physiological bases of emotion, Lund published two important books on the psychology of emotion (1930 and 1939), establishing himself as the leading authority in the field. He also became expert on the emotional adjustment of children in the classroom. His many publications on that topic led to considerable fame within the education profession.[12]

Grace Esther Munson (1883–1980)

Munson was born on October 17, 1883, in Orleans, Nebraska. After teaching for four years in schools in Geneva, Nebraska, she earned her A.B. degree in philosophy at the University of Nebraska in 1911 and her Ph.D. in education, also at Nebraska, in 1916. She worked with both Wolfe and Luckey and was strongly influenced by their emphases on child study. After graduation she joined the Bureau of Child Study in Chicago as a psychologist. She remained in that position until 1935, when she became a school psychologist with the Joyce Kilmer Experimental School in Chicago. During her tenure in that job she was elected a fellow of the American Psychological Association.

Toward the end of her career, Munson was employed by the Chicago Board of Education as an assistant superintendent for special education. She retired in 1949. Her few publications dealt with the field of child study.

Walter Bowers Pillsbury (1872–1960)

Pillsbury, born on July 21, 1872, in Burlington, Iowa, was the first of Wolfe's undergraduates to take his doctorate in psychology and, with the possible exception of Edwin Guthrie, was Wolfe's most famous student. Pillsbury transferred to the University of Nebraska in 1890 after two years at Penn College in Iowa and completed his A.B. with Wolfe in 1892. After a year of teaching at Grand Island College in Nebraska, he accepted a fellowship for graduate study at Cornell University. There he became E. B. Titchener's second doctoral student, completing the degree in 1896. He rejected Wolfe's offer of an instructorship at Nebraska in 1896 (see chapter 5) and instead accepted Titchener's offer of a postdoctoral assistantship at Cornell.

In 1897 the University of Michigan offered, and Pillsbury accepted, the chair in psychology and the opportunity to establish a new laboratory in psychology. At the same time, G. Stanley Hall invited him to become a cooperating editor on his journal, the *American Journal of Psychology*.

Pillsbury was the director of the psychology laboratory at Michigan throughout his long tenure there. In 1929, when psychology was made a department separate from philosophy, Pillsbury was made the head of the department, a post he held until his retirement in 1942, after forty-five years at Michigan.

Sixty-five students earned doctoral degrees in psychology during Pillsbury's years at Michigan, and he chaired twenty-three of those dissertations. Most of the others were chaired by John F. Shepard, Pillsbury's first doctoral student, who stayed on the Michigan faculty.

Pillsbury's publications numbered about one hundred, seventeen of which were books. His scholarship was broad, leading to books on reasoning (1910), educational theory (1925), the psychology of language (1928), and the history of psychology (1929). His most famous work was a book on attention, which was originally published in French (1906) and later in English (1908). Some of his books were textbooks that went through several editions. In addition to his writing, he served as either cooperating editor or coeditor of the *American Journal of Psychology* for an incredible sixty-three years.

Not surprisingly, Pillsbury's honors were numerous. He was elected president of the Western Philosophical Association in 1907 and president of the American Psychological Association in 1910. In 1925 he was elected a member of the prestigious National Academy of Science. The University of Nebraska conferred an honorary doctoral degree on him in 1933. When the 1939 annual meeting of the Midwestern Psychological Association was held on the University of Nebraska campus in conjunction with the celebration of the fiftieth anniversary of the founding of Wolfe's laboratory, Pillsbury presented an invited address on Wolfe.[13]

Donald Fox Showalter (1891–1972)

Showalter was born on May 4, 1891, in Davenport, Nebraska. He earned his A.B. in 1916 and his A.M. in 1917 at the University of Nebraska, serving the last year as Wolfe's laboratory assistant. He taught in high schools, and for a year at the Kansas State Teachers College in Emporia (1924), before pursuing his doctoral work at the University of Kansas. He received his Ph.D. there in 1931. Showalter spent the next fifteen years at the State Agricultural and Mechanical College of Arkansas (Jonesboro) as the head of the Department of Education. For a year he served as the acting president of the college.

In 1947, Showalter joined the faculty of Kansas State College in Manhattan. His few publications were in the field of educational psychology on the subjects of educational tests and measurements.

Hazel Martha Stanton (1890–1977)

Stanton was born in Stromsburg, Nebraska, on July 16, 1890. She completed her A.B. degree at the University of Nebraska in 1912 and her Ph.D. at the University of Iowa in 1921. She was principally influenced by Carl Emil Seashore at Iowa (see earlier listing for William Severt Larson) and pursued his interests in the psychology of music.

In 1921, Stanton joined the faculty of the Eastman School of Music as a professor of psychology. There, following Seashore's work, she helped develop music tests that were used for students seeking admission to Eastman. Her publications included works on the inheritance of musical ability, the prediction of musical progress, gifted children and music, and the measurement of musical capacity. Her one book, *Psychology in Education*, was published in 1941.

Stanton stayed at Eastman until 1943, when she took a job with a psychological consulting firm, Daniel Starch and Associates. The company was based in New York, but Stanton was made the Northwest Regional Manager at the company's office in Portland, Oregon. She held that job until her retirement. Stanton was listed in *Who's Who in American Women*.

Carl John Warden (1890–1961)

Born in Hamilton, Missouri, on March 18, 1890, Warden completed his undergraduate work in 1915 at Cotner College in

Bethany, Nebraska, now a part of the city of Lincoln. He studied with Wolfe for a year, earning his A.M. degree from Nebraska in 1916, and then pursued his doctoral study at the University of Chicago, finishing there in 1922.

After graduation, Warden accepted a position at the University of Wisconsin but was there only a year before joining the
faculty at Columbia University. Warden achieved considerable
recognition as one of America's important early comparative
psychologists, publishing four books on the topic, three of
those with Thomas N. Jenkins (see earlier listing). He was the
inventor of a widely used piece of apparatus called the Columbia Obstruction Box, a device used to measure the relative
strengths of competing motivational states by forcing an animal to cross an electrified grid to achieve a desired goal.

Warden also conducted research in social psychology, publishing *The Emergence of Human Culture* in 1936. He trained a
large number of doctoral students during his thirty-three years
at Columbia, retiring in 1955.

Christian Oliver Weber (1892–1982)

Weber was born in Friend, Nebraska, on December 10, 1892. He
earned an A.B. degree in 1916 and an A.M. degree in 1918 from
the University of Nebraska. In 1920 he was hired as an instructor
in philosophy and for two years taught courses in applied psychology (later he changed the title to industrial psychology), in
addition to several philosophy courses. His doctoral work was
completed in psychology at Harvard University in 1924.

Weber joined the faculty at Wells College in Aurora, New
York, in 1925 and remained there until his retirement in 1958. His
publications are a mix of child study (play, moral judgment, emotion, delinquency, mental deficiency), industrial psychology
(business psychology, industrial creativity, job testing), and perception (kinesthesis, movement). He established himself principally as an educational psychologist, writing a book on reading
(1951) and another on educational philosophy (1960).

When Samuel Fernberger identified Nebraska as the third
leading source of inspiration for psychology among the mem-

bers of the American Psychological Association during the 1920s, not all of those claiming Nebraska roots were Wolfe's students.[14] Among those early Nebraskans who became psychologists but did not study with Wolfe were the fourth and fifth Nebraska undergraduates to serve as president of the American Psychological Association (APA).

Harry Levi Hollingworth (1880–1956), a native of DeWitt, Nebraska, finished his A.B. degree at the university in 1906 with Thaddeus L. Bolton and his doctorate in psychology at Columbia University in 1909 with Cattell, Edward L. Thorndike, and Robert S. Woodworth. He spent his entire career on the faculty of Columbia University's Barnard College. His publications included more than twenty books and one hundred articles, most of them on psychology applied to business, industry, and education. He was elected APA president in 1927.[15]

Harry Hollingworth's wife was also a prominent psychologist. Leta Anna Stetter was born in Dawes County, Nebraska, in 1886. She too studied with Bolton, finishing at the University of Nebraska in 1906. Two years later she married her classmate in New York City. Leta Hollingworth (1886–1939) earned her doctorate from Columbia University in 1916, working with Thorndike. As a member of the faculty of Columbia University's Teachers College, she became perhaps the best-known female psychologist of her day for her work in the psychology of sex differences and adolescence, and she was recognized internationally as one of the leaders in the field of gifted education. She and her husband received honorary doctoral degrees from the University of Nebraska in 1938. The following year, at the age of fifty-three, Leta Hollingworth died of cancer.[16]

The fifth APA president from the University of Nebraska was Joy Paul Guilford (1897–1987) from Marquette, Nebraska. Guilford studied at Nebraska with Winifred Hyde and earned his A.B. and A.M. degrees. After completing his doctorate in psychology at Cornell University, he spent his academic career at the University of Nebraska (1928–40) and the University of Southern California (1940–62). His more than three hundred scientific publications include many on the subject of intelligence, and his "Structure of Intellect" model remains an important theory of intelligence in contemporary psychology.

His many honors include the election to the presidency of the APA in 1950, an honorary degree from the University of Nebraska in 1952, and the Gold Medal Award from the American Psychological Foundation in 1983.[17]

Guilford was the mentor for another Nebraska undergraduate who became president of the APA, in 1952. Joseph McVicker Hunt was born in Scottsbluff, Nebraska, in 1906. (His father, Robert Sanford Hunt, had been one of Wolfe's undergraduates, Class of 1899, and had planned to go to Leipzig to study with Wundt. But an illness in his senior year left him partially deaf, and he felt he would not be able to do well in lecture classes conducted in German.)[18] J. McV. Hunt earned his A.B. degree at Nebraska in 1929 and his doctorate in psychology at Cornell University in 1933. Following a decade at Brown University and five years as the director of the Institute of Welfare Research, he has spent most of his career at the University of Illinois. In 1961 he wrote *Intelligence and Experience*, a book that was largely responsible for the initiation of the Project Head Start Program of President John F. Kennedy. Hunt received an honorary doctorate from the University of Nebraska in 1967.[19]

When Hunt was elected to the APA presidency in 1952, he was the sixth University of Nebraska undergraduate to hold that honor. At that time only two other universities could claim more than two presidents: the University of California counted four of its undergraduates among the APA presidents, and the University of Michigan had three.[20] Although the University of California has since added two more, to bring its total to six as well, Nebraska's leadership as the most prolific nursery for presidents of the APA remains unsurpassed today.

Wolfe's first undergraduate students who would become presidents of the American Psychological Association were Walter Pillsbury (left) and Madison Bentley. (Photos courtesy of the Archives of the History of American Psychology)

Notes

Chapter 1: The Making of a Teacher

1. For an excellent volume of essays on Wilhelm Wundt, see Bringmann, Wolfgang G., & Tweney, Ryan D. (Eds.). *Wundt Studies: A Centennial Collection.* Toronto: C. J. Hogrefe, 1980.

2. See, for example, Garvey, C. R. List of American psychology laboratories. *Psychological Bulletin,* 1929, *26,* 652–660.

3. Leacock, Stephen. A manual for the new mentality. *Harpers,* March 1924, p. 471; Benjamin, Ludy T., Jr. Why don't they understand us: A history of psychology's public image. *American Psychologist,* 1986, *41,* 941–946.

4. Wiggam, A. E. *Exploring Your Mind with the Psychologists.* New York: Bobbs Merrill, 1928, p. 13.

5. Evans, Rand B., & Scott, F. J. D. The 1913 International Congress of Psychology: The American congress that wasn't. *American Psychologist,* 1978, *33,* 711–723.

6. Sokal, Michael M. First U. S. International Congress. *APA Monitor,* July/August 1979, p. 3.

7. Cattell, James McKeen. Psychology in America. *Science,* 1929, *70,* 339. The 1929 congress was described in some detail in *Time* magazine. See "Psychologists," *Time,* September 16, 1929, pp. 52–55.

8. Fernberger, Samuel W. Further statistics of the American Psychological Association. *Psychological Bulletin,* 1921, *18,* 569–572; Fernberger, S. W. Statistical analyses of the members and associates of the American Psychological Association, Inc. *Psychological Review,* 1928, *35,* 447–465.

9. Sources differ on the number of American students who actually took a doctoral degree with Wundt at Leipzig. Based on student records at the University of Leipzig, thirty-three Ameri-

cans had their dissertations signed by Wundt. Of that number, sixteen listed Wundt as major professor (*Erstgutachter*). Thirteen of the sixteen did their dissertation research in psychology; the other three wrote philosophical dissertations.

10   Wedded for fifty years. *Nebraska State Journal* (Lincoln), December 18, 1907, p. 5.

11   After farming in Nebraska for more than twenty-five years, Jacob Wolfe returned to politics once more. For four years he served as Nebraska's commissioner of public lands. Leasing such lands provided most of the revenue for many local school districts, and during his two terms of office, Wolfe greatly increased school revenue by collecting from individuals and corporations that had been habitually delinquent in their payments. In 1892, he was state chairman of the Populist party in Nebraska, a party that had grown from the farmers' disenchantment with the two established political parties. The Populists enjoyed limited success in Nebraska, electing governors for three terms in the 1890s. See Trask, David S. A natural partnership: Nebraska's Populists and Democrats and the development of fusion. *Nebraska History*, 1975, *56*, 418–438. Jacob Wolfe was also a strong supporter of William Jennings Bryan. Their farms were adjacent and they worked together in Nebraska politics. When Jacob Wolfe died in 1913, Bryan, then secretary of state under Woodrow Wilson, wrote to H. K. Wolfe to express his sorrow at losing an "intimate friend." Letter located in the Wolfe Family Papers, Friday Harbor, Washington (hereafter cited as WFP).

12   Wedded for fifty years, p. 5.

13   On hearing her father talk about reading Latin while he walked behind a plow, Isabel, Wolfe's older daughter, said she always wondered how straight the furrows were. Isabel Wolfe Hemenway, interview with author, 1981.

14   Caldwell, Howard W. An introduction to the history of higher education in Nebraska, and a brief account of the University of Nebraska. *Transactions and Reports of the Nebraska State Historical Society*, 1892, *3*, 201–229.

15   Manley, Robert N. *Centennial History of the University of Nebraska, I: Frontier University, 1869–1919.* Lincoln: University of Nebraska Press, 1969.

16   Day, Jeremiah. Original paper in relation to a course of liberal education. *American Journal of Science and Arts*, 1829, *15*, 300–301. Cited in Watson, Robert I., *The Great Psychologists* (4th ed.). Philadelphia: Lippincott, 1978, p. 368.

17   H. K. Wolfe's undergraduate transcript for the years 1876–1880 was made available by the Registrar's Office, University of Nebraska, with the permission of the Wolfe family.

18   Caldwell, An introduction to the history of higher education, p. 223.

19   Manley, *Centennial History,* pp. 59–61, 69–75.

20   The University of Nebraska radically altered its curriculum in the fall of 1880, the year after Wolfe's graduation, permitting students to pursue a number of programs of study. The university introduced the new curriculum as follows: "The elective system is the one that insures the greatest interest and profit in every study, and it is the only system that allows a student to become a special scholar in any one department while still leaving to him the option of a general education." Caldwell, An introduction to the history of higher education, p. 217.

21   Fay, Jay W. *American Psychology before William James.* New Brunswick, NJ: Rutgers University Press, 1939; Evans, Rand B. The origin of American academic psychology. In J. Brozek (Ed.), *Explorations in the History of Psychology in the United States.* Lewisburg, PA: Bucknell University Press, 1984.

22   Description of courses in "Intellectual, Moral, and Political Philosophy." University of Nebraska Catalog, October 1879, p. 14. University of Nebraska–Lincoln Archives (hereafter cited as UNA).

23   Leahey, Thomas H. *A History of Psychology: Main Currents in Psychological Thought.* (2nd ed.). New York: Prentice Hall, 1987, p. 251.

24   A surprise party. Newspaper clipping (newspaper not identified) November 10, 1879. WFP.

25   Commencement Exercises. Newspaper clipping (newspaper not identified) June 9, 1880. WFP.

26   University Commencement. *Daily State Journal* (Lincoln), June 10, 1880, pp. 1, 4.

27   Manley, *Centennial History,* p. 48.

28   Ibid., pp. 47–53.

29   Wolff, Christian von. *Psychologia Empirica* (1732) and *Psychologia Rationalis* (1734). Frankfurt: Rengeriana. See Richards, Robert J. Christian Wolff's prolegomena to empirical and rational psychology: Translation and commentary. *Proceedings of the American Philosophical Society,* 1980, *124,* 227–239.

30   Commencement exercises. Of Wolfe's classmates, Howard Caldwell would become a faculty member in the Department of

History at the University of Nebraska, Emma Parks (Wilson) would become the university's first Dean of Women, David H. Mercer would be elected to the U.S. House of Representatives from Nebraska, and J. H. Worley would serve as a missionary in China.

Chapter 2: Germany and the New Psychology

Three sources were particularly important for this chapter. One was a set of extensive interviews conducted with Isabel Wolfe Hemenway, Katharine A. Wolfe, and Harry Kirke Wolfe II in 1981. Second are Wolfe's notebooks, ledger, and registration book from his study in Berlin (1883–84) and Leipzig (1884–86), which are part of the Wolfe Family Papers (WFP) in Friday Harbor, Washington. Finally, because there are no letters existing from Wolfe's study in Germany, Michael Sokal's edited volume of the letters of James McKeen Cattell (a contemporary of Wolfe's at Leipzig) was especially important in providing a sense of Wundt's laboratory at that time.

1   For a discussion of the founding of the University of Berlin, see Fallon, Daniel. *The German University: A Heroic Ideal in Conflict with the Modern World*. Boulder: Colorado Associated Universities Press, 1980, chapter 3.

2   See Thwing, Charles. *The Americans and the German University: One Hundred Years of History*. New York: Macmillan, 1928; Bonner, Thomas N. *American Doctors and German Universities: A Chapter in International Intellectual Relations, 1879–1914*. Lincoln: University of Nebraska Press, 1963; Herbst, Jurgen. *The German Historical School in American Scholarship: A Study in the Transfer of Ideas*. Ithaca, NY: Cornell University Press, 1965.

3   Bruce, Robert V. *The Launching of Modern American Science, 1846–1876*. Ithaca, NY: Cornell University Press, 1987.

4   Registration book for Harry Kirke Wolfe at Friedrich Wilhelm University of Berlin, 1883–84. WFP.

5   Ledger of Harry Kirke Wolfe, 1883–86. WFP.

6   Registration book, Berlin. WFP.

7   Traxel, Werner. Hermann Ebbinghaus: In memoriam. *History of Psychology Newsletter* (APA Division 26), 1985, 17, 37–41. See Fallon, *The German University*, pp. 41–43, for a discussion of the German academic concept of habilitation.

8   Ebbinghaus, Hermann. *Über das Gedächtnis*. Leipzig: Von Duncker and Humblot, 1885. English translation by Henry A. Ruger,

New York: Teachers College Press, 1913.

9 Fechner, Gustav T. *Elemente der Psychophysik*. Leipzig: Briet Kopf and Hartel, 1860. English translation by Helmut Adler, New York: Holt, Rinehart and Winston, 1966.

10 Shakow, David. Hermann Ebbinghaus. *American Journal of Psychology*, 1930, 42, 505–518.

11 Titchener, Edward B. *A Text-book of Psychology*. New York: Macmillan, 1928, p. 125.

12 Hoffman, Robert R., Klein, Richard, & Bamberg, Michael. Some historical observations on Ebbinghaus. In D. Gorfein & R. Hoffman (Eds.), *Learning and Memory: The Ebbinghaus Centennial Conference*. Hillsdale, NJ: Lawrence Erlbaum, 1986.

13 James, William. Experiments in memory. *Science*, 1885, 6, 198–199. See also James, W. *Talks to Teachers and Students*. New York: Holt, 1899, p. 139.

14 Schultz, Duane, & Schultz, Sydney Ellen. *A History of Modern Psychology* (4th ed.). San Diego: Harcourt, Brace, Jovanovich, 1987, p. 73.

15 Wolfe, H. K. Notes from Ebbinghaus's psychology class, April 28, 1884, p. 1. WFP.

16 Ebbinghaus, Hermann. *Abriss der Psychologie*. Leipzig: Veit, 1910.

17 Wolfe, H. K. Notes from Ebbinghaus, p. 11. WFP.

18 Wolfe's registration book does not indicate that he took any summer classes at Berlin in 1884; however, his papers contain notes from a course entitled "Modern Philosophy in Connection with Modern Culture" and dated May–July 1884, Berlin. WFP.

19 The publication of Ebbinghaus's book in 1885 earned him an associate professorship at Berlin in 1886. After that book, Ebbinghaus published little at Berlin. He was not promoted, and he left Berlin in 1894 for a lesser position in Breslau. In 1905 he joined the faculty at the University of Halle, where he died of pneumonia in 1909, at the age of fifty-nine.

20 Sokal, Michael M. (Ed.). *An Education in Psychology: James McKeen Cattell's Journal and Letters from Germany and England, 1880–1888*. Cambridge, MA: MIT Press, 1981, p. 11. G. Stanley Hall was the first American to study in Wundt's laboratory, visiting there in 1879. However, Hall took no degree there and actually spent most of his time working with Carl Ludwig in physiology. See Bringmann, Norma J., & Bringmann, Wolfgang G. Wilhelm Wundt and his first American student. In Wolfgang G.

Bringmann & Ryan D. Tweney (Eds.), *Wundt Studies: A Centennial Collection.* Toronto: C. J. Hogrefe, 1980, pp. 176–192.

21 Sokal, *An Education in Psychology,* p. 136. Cattell's letter is dated October 28, 1884.

22 For an account of the twenty-eight years Wundt spent in Heidelberg, see Bringmann, Wolfgang G. Wundt in Heidelberg, 1845–1874. *Canadian Psychological Review,* 1975, *16,* 116–121.

23 Bringman & Tweney, *Wundt Studies,* is an excellent source of information on Wundt. See also Blumenthal, Arthur L. A reappraisal of Wilhelm Wundt. *American Psychologist,* 1975, *30,* 1081–1088.

24 For a listing of 186 philosophy and psychology doctoral students of Wundt's, see Tinker, Miles A. Wundt's doctorate students and their theses: 1875–1920. *American Journal of Psychology,* 1932, *44,* 630–637. The countries of origin of those students are included in Doktoranden Wilhelm Wundts. *Wissenschaftliche Zeitschrift: Karl Marx Universitat–Leipzig,* 1980, *2,* 161–166.

25 Danziger, Kurt. The history of introspection reconsidered. *Journal of the History of the Behavioral Sciences,* 1980, *16,* 241–262.

26 Wolfe, H. K. German influences on psychology. Undated notes (probably written around 1900), pp. 2–3. WFP.

27 For a description of the psychological research in the early days of Wundt's laboratory, see Cattell, James McK. The psychological laboratory at Leipsic. *Mind,* 1888, *13,* 37–51.

28 Wundt, W. *Grundriss der Psychologie.* Leipzig: Engelmann, 1896. From Judd, Charles H. (Trans.). *Outlines of Psychology.* New York: Gustav Sechert, 1902, p. 103.

29 Baldwin, Bird T. In memory of Wilhelm Wundt. *Psychological Review,* 1921, *28,* 153–188.

30 Berliner, Anna. Reminiscences of Wundt and Leipzig. January 1959, 9 pp. Berliner Papers, Archives of the History of American Psychology, University of Akron, Ohio.

31 Meischner, Wolfram, & Metge, Anneros. *Zur Geschichte des Psychologischen Denkens an der Universitat Leipzig.* Leipzig: Karl-Marx University, 1985. See page 43 for a listing of these courses.

32 Baldwin, In memory of Wilhelm Wundt. See letter from G. A. Tawney, pp. 178–181.

33 Ibid., letter from Titchener, pp. 162–163.

34 Sokal, *An Education in Psychology,* p. 89.

35 Ibid., p. 141. Cattell wrote to his parents on November 15, 1884: "I have found a new psychologist—a very good man, named

Wolfe from Nebraska. He wants to pass his examination here in psychology and afterwards to teach it. He is coming to me two evenings a week to be experimented on, and would come oftener if I needed him."

36 Wolfe, H. K. Ledger, 1883–86. WFP.

37 The other memory dissertations were by Zwetan Radoslawow-Hadjidenkow (1899) and Carl Jesinghaus (1912).

38 Robinson, David K. Wundt and Ebbinghaus: What the letters say. *History of Psychology Newsletter* (APA Division 26), 1985, 17, 46–50.

39 Although popularized by Fechner, this method, also called the method of right and wrong cases, was developed in 1852 by Karl von Vierordt (1818–84), a physiologist at Tübingen.

40 Wolfe, H. K. Notes on memory, etc., Leipzig 1885. 26 pp. WFP. Apparently this was a literature review in preparation for his dissertation.

41 Stumpf's *Tonpsychologie* was published in two volumes, the first in 1883 and the second in 1890. Helmholtz's *Lehre von den Tonempfindungen als physiologischen Grundlage für die Theorie der Musik* was published in 1863 and revised through 1877.

42 One of the subjects in Wolfe's research was the famous Russian physiologist Vladimir M. Bekhterev (1857–1927). Bekhterev earned his medical degree in St. Petersburg in 1881 and was working in Wundt's laboratory at the time Wolfe was there.

43 Wolfe, H. K. Untersuchungen über das Tongedächtniss. *Philosophische Studien*, 1886, 3, 534–571.

44 Jastrow's reviews appeared in *Science*, 1886, 6, 459–460, and *American Journal of Psychology*, 1887, 1, 185–186.

45 James, William. *Principles of Psychology* (2 vols.). New York: Henry Holt, 1890, see p. 639.

46 Boring, Edwin G. *A History of Experimental Psychology* (2nd ed.). New York: Appleton-Century-Crofts, 1950, p. 340. Wundt and Stumpf waged a somewhat acrimonius dispute in the scientific literature on the psychology of tone, a battle begun when Stumpf criticized a dissertation by one of Wundt's students (Carl Lorenz). Stumpf argued the correctness of his position on the basis of judgments made by expert musicians; Wundt countered that musical "bias" was eliminated in his laboratory studies employing precise measures. See Boring, E. G. The psychology of controversy. *Psychological Review*, 1929, 36, 107–113.

47 One of the contributions of Müller and Schumann was the invention of the memory drum, a device that was popular in psy-

chological research for much of the twentieth century.

48   Boring, *A History of Experimental Psychology*, p. 343.

49   Letter from James McKeen Cattell to his parents, April 18, 1886. Cattell Papers, Manuscript Collections, Library of Congress, Washington DC.

50   Letter from Wilhelm Wundt, November 16, 1886. Translated by Laurence Fossler. WFP. Wundt's letter for Cattell is much more detailed and glowing in its content. For Cattell's letter, see Sokal, *An Education in Psychology*, p. 175.

51   Letters of recommendation for public school jobs and a position at the University of Wisconsin, dated 1887. WFP.

52   Katharine Brandt Wolfe's early experience with tutors may later have suggested to her the practice of tutoring her children to supplement their primary school education, a practice that resulted in two graduating from high school at the age of fifteen and one graduating at fourteen.

53   Isabel Wolfe Hemenway, interview with author, 1981.

Chapter 3: Mental States and Sugar Beets

This chapter relies heavily on two sources: (1) correspondence and lecture notes of H. K. Wolfe (Wolfe Papers) and the papers of the board of regents, both in the University of Nebraska Archives (UNA), and (2) correspondence and lecture notes in the Wolfe Family Papers (WFP).

1   Olson, James C. *History of Nebraska* (2nd ed.). Lincoln: University of Nebraska Press, 1966, chapter 17: The eighties, whose prosperity?

2   Manley, Robert N. *Centennial History of the University of Nebraska, I: Frontier University, 1869–1919*. Lincoln: University of Nebraska Press, 1969. See especially pp. 34–41 and 108–110.

3   Cattell, James McK. Early psychological laboratories. *Science*, 1928, *67*, 543–548; Garvey, C. R. List of American psychology laboratories. *Psychological Bulletin*, 1929, *26*, 652–660; Murray, Frank S., & Rowe, Frederick B. Psychology laboratories in the United States prior to 1900. *Teaching of Psychology*, 1979, *6*, 19–21; Ruckmich, Christian A. The history and status of psychology in the United States. *American Journal of Psychology*, 1912, *23*, 517–531. All four sources list the University of Nebraska's psychology laboratory as the sixth founded in the United States. Earlier labs were founded at Harvard, Johns Hopkins, Indiana, Pennsylvania, and Wisconsin. Psychology as a laboratory science fol-

lowed closely on the heels of other laboratory sciences in America. See Bruce, Robert V. *The Launching of Modern American Science, 1846–1876*. Ithaca, NY: Cornell University Press, 1987.

4   Wolfe, Harry K. On the color-vocabulary of children. *University Studies* (Nebraska), 1890, *1*, 205–234. See also, Wolfe, H. K. Observations on the study of children. *Education*, 1890, *11*, 201–207.

5   Letter from H. K. Wolfe to C. E. Bessey, May 15, 1890. Annual report of the Department of Philosophy. Board of Regents Papers, UNA.

6   Ibid., pp. 1–2; see also Wolfe, H. K. Psychology at the University of Nebraska. *American Journal of Psychology*, 1890, *3*, 276–277.

7   Brochure, An exhibit in honor of the 75th anniversary of the American Psychological Association, 1967. Available from the Archives of the History of American Psychology, University of Akron, Ohio.

8   Wolfe to Bessey, May 15, 1890, annual report, pp. 1, 4. Board of Regents Papers, UNA.

9   Ibid., p. 4.

10   Letter from H. K. Wolfe to the board of regents, June 12, 1890. Board of Regents Papers, UNA.

11   Letter from H. K. Wolfe to the board of regents, June 10, 1890. Board of Regents Papers, UNA.

12   Letter from H. K. Wolfe to the board of regents, May 29, 1891. Annual report of the Department of Philosophy, p. 3. Board of Regents Papers, UNA.

13   Ibid., p. 1.

14   Ibid., p. 7.

15   Letter from H. K. Wolfe to the board of regents, May ?, 1891. See also letter from H. K. Wolfe to the board of regents, April 7, 1891. Board of Regents Papers, UNA.

16   Anderson, O. E. *The Health of a Nation: Harvey W. Wiley and the Fight for Pure Food*. Chicago: University of Chicago Press, 1958; Brown, Sara A., & Sargent, Robie O. Children in the sugar beet fields of the North Platte Valley of Nebraska, 1923. *Nebraska History*, 1986, *67*, 256–303. Wolfe's brothers William and Vance, both of whom earned degrees in chemistry from the University of Nebraska, worked in a sugar beet factory for a few years before returning to farming.

17   Anthropometric mental testing was begun by Sir Francis Galton, the founder of the science of eugenics and a first cousin of Charles Darwin, and was championed in the United States by James McK. Cattell. By 1900 it had been largely discredited, the

deathblow dealt by one of Cattell's own students when it was shown that correlations between these tests and academic performance was virtually zero. See Sokal, Michael M. James McKeen Cattell and the failure of anthropometric mental testing, 1890–1901. In W. R. Woodward & M. G. Ash (Eds.), *The Problematic Science: Psychology in Nineteenth-Century Thought.* New York: Praeger, 1982, pp. 322–345.

18 Wolfe to the regents, May 29, 1891, annual report. Board of Regents Papers, UNA

19 Letter from H. K. Wolfe to the chancellor and board of regents, April 11, 1893. Board of Regents Papers, UNA.

20 Manley, *Centennial History,* chapter 11: The 1890s: A time of decision, and chapter 12: Public education and academic developments; Gappa, LaVon M. Chancellor James Hulme Canfield: His impact on the University of Nebraska, 1891–1895. *Nebraska History,* 1985, *66,* 392–410. For a history of the normal college at Peru, Nebraska, see Young, Kenneth. A history of Peru Normal. *Nebraska History,* 1932, *13,* 86–95.

21 Letter from H. K. Wolfe to the chancellor and board of regents, March 31, 1895. Annual Report of the Department of Philosophy, p. 1. Board of Regents Papers, UNA. The student was Walter Bowers Pillsbury, an 1892 graduate of the University of Nebraska, who, at the time of his writing, was working on his doctorate in psychology with Edward Bradford Titchener, another of Wundt's graduates. Pillsbury was later head of the Department of Psychology at the University of Michigan and a president of the American Psychological Association. See biographical sketch in the Appendix.

22 Wolfe to the chancellor and regents, March 31, 1895, annual report pp. 2, 3. Board of Regents Papers, UNA.

23 Letter from H. K. Wolfe to Walter B. Pillsbury, August 8, 1894. Pillsbury Papers, Michigan Historical Collections, Bentley Historical Library, University of Michigan, Ann Arbor.

24 Wolfe to the chancellor and regents, March 31, 1895, annual report, p. 4, Board of Regents Papers, UNA.

25 Wolfe, Harry K. The new psychology in undergraduate work. *Psychological Review,* 1895, *2,* 382–387.

26 French, Ferdinand C. The place of experimental psychology in the undergraduate course. *Psychological Review,* 1898, *5,* 510–512.

27 Billia, Lorenzo M. Has the psychological laboratory proved helpful? *Monist,* July 1909, pp. 351–366.

28   Napoli, Donald S. *Architects of Adjustment: The History of the Psy-
      chological Profession in the United States*. Port Washington, NY:
      Kennikat Press, 1981; Fernberger, Samuel W. Further statistics
      of the American Psychological Association. *Psychological Bulle-
      tin*, 1921, *18*, 569–572.

29   Many of the student research projects in child study were pub-
      lished in the *North Western Journal of Education*, a locally pub-
      lished journal for which Luckey and Wolfe served as associate
      editors.

30   Letter from H. K. Wolfe to board of regents, March 24, 1897, p. 1.
      Board of Regents Papers, UNA.

31   Remarks by Hartley Burr Alexander at the funeral service for
      Wolfe, August 3, 1918. WFP.

32   These comments are based on a collection of more than seventy
      of Wolfe's unpublished lectures in both the WFP and UNA.

33   Wolfe, H. K. *The psychology of research*, p. 1. Unpublished lecture.
      Wolfe Papers, UNA.

34   Ibid., p. 9.

35   Ibid., p. 14

36   See Fernberger, further statistics; Fernberger, S. W. Statistical
      analyses of the members and associates of the American Psy-
      chological Association, Inc. *Psychological Review,* 1928, *35*, 447–
      465. Wolfe's students are discussed in the Appendix.

37   Wolfe, H. K. *The data of psychology,* p. 30. Unpublished lecture.
      Wolfe Papers, UNA.

38   Letter from H. K. Wolfe to Walter B. Pillsbury, November 2,
      1895. Pillsbury Papers.

39   Davidson, Emily S., & Benjamin, Ludy T., Jr. A history of the
      child study movement. In J. Glover & R. Ronning (Eds.), *Histor-
      ical Foundations of Educational Psychology*. New York: Plenum
      Press, 1987, pp. 41–60.

40   Letter from H. K. Wolfe to the chancellor and board of regents,
      April 11, 1891. Board of Regents Papers, UNA.

Chapter 4: Scientific Pedagogy

Portions of this chapter are taken from Emily S. Davidson and
Ludy T. Benjamin, Jr., "A History of the Child Study Movement in
America," in John A. Glover and Royce R. Ronning (Eds.), *Histori-
cal Foundations of Educational Psychology* (New York: Plenum Press,
1987), pp. 41–60. The author gratefully acknowledges Emily
Davidson's and Plenum Press's permission to use this material.

1 Sahakian, Mabel L., & Sahakian, William S. *Rousseau as Educator*. New York: Twayne, 1974.

2 Downs, R. B. *Heinrich Pestalozzi*. Boston, MA: Twayne, 1975.

3 Downs, R. B. *Friedrich Froebel*. Boston, MA: Twayne, 1978.

4 Dunkel, H. B. *Herbart and Herbartianism*. Chicago: University of Chicago Press, 1970.

5 Pounds, R. L. *The Development of Education in Western Culture*. New York: Appleton-Century-Crofts, 1968; Olson, James C. *History of Nebraska* (2nd ed.). Lincoln: University of Nebraska Press, 1966, p. 345.

6 Dennis, Wayne. Historical beginnings of child psychology. *Psychological Bulletin*, 1949, 46, 224–235.

7 Ross, Dorothy. *G. Stanley Hall: The Psychologist as Prophet*. Chicago: University of Chicago Press, 1972, p. 127.

8 Hall, G. Stanley. The contents of children's minds. *Princeton Review*, 1883, 2, 249–272; Hendricks, J. D. *The child study movement in American education, 1880–1910: A quest for educational reform through a systematic study of the child*. Unpublished doctoral dissertation, Indiana University, Bloomington, 1968.

9 Wolfe, Harry K. Historical sketch of child study. *North Western Journal of Education*, 1896, 7, 9–12. Wolfe's interest in the quality of the school environment for children was shared by his wife, Katharine. She wrote several articles on the subject and pursued those concerns when she worked for the Lincoln Public Schools as a school physician from 1918 to 1925.

10 Ross, *G. Stanley Hall*. See especially the three chapters on the child study movement, chapters 15–17.

11 Hall, G. Stanley. The new psychology as a basis of education. *Forum*, 1894, 17, 710–720; Winship, A. E. Why child study? *Journal of Education*, 1892, 36, 141; Wolfe, Harry K. *The theory of child study*. Unpublished lecture. Wolfe Papers, UNA. See also Schlossman, S. L. Before home start: Notes toward a history of parent education. *Harvard Educational Review*, 1976, 46, 436–467.

12 Wolfe, H. K. *The data of psychology*. Unpublished lecture. Wolfe Papers, UNA.

13 Hall, G. Stanley. Child study at Clark University. *American Journal of Psychology*, 1903, 14, 96–106; Hall, G. S. *Life and Confessions of a Psychologist*. New York: Appleton, 1923.

14 Wolfe, H. K. Observations on the study of children. *Education*, 1890, 11, 201–207.

15 Wolfe, Harry K. On the color-vocabulary of children. *University Studies* (Nebraska), 1890, 1, 205–234.

16   Wolfe, Harry K. The state societies for child study. *North Western Journal of Education*, 1896, *7*, 45.

17   Wolfe, Harry K. Notes on educational method. *Educational Review*, 1892, *4*, 29.

18   Ibid., p. 30.

19   Baldwin, James M. Child study. *Psychological Review*, 1898, *5*, 219. See also, Baldwin, J. M. *Mental Development in the Child and Race: Methods and Processes*. New York: Macmillan, 1895.

20   Münsterberg, Hugo. The danger from experimental psychology. *Atlantic Monthly*, 1898, *81*, 166.

21   Münsterberg, Hugo. Psychology and education. *Education Review*, 1898, *16*, 114; idem, The danger from experimental psychology, p. 165.

22   Münsterberg, Psychology and education, pp. 114–115.

23   See, for example, Bliss, C. B. Professor Münsterberg's attack on experimental psychology. *Forum*, 1898, *25*, 214–223; Davies, H. The teacher's attitude toward psychology. *Education*, 1899, *19*, 476–485.

24   Hall, G. Stanley. Child study and its relation to education. *Forum*, 1900, *29*, 692.

25   Ibid., p. 693.

26   Wolfe, *The data of psychology*. Wolfe Papers. UNA. William James's concerns were that teachers were being pressured into participating in child study work. He wrote:

> Least of all need you, merely *as teachers*, deem it part of your duty to become contributors to psychological science or to make psychological observations in a methodical or responsible manner. I fear that some of the enthusiasts for child-study have thrown a certain burden on you in this way. By all means let child-study go on,—it is refreshing all our sense of the child's life. There are teachers who take a spontaneous delight in filling syllabuses, inscribing observations, compiling statistics, and computing the per cent. Child study will certainly enrich their lives. . . . But, for Heaven's sake, let the rank and file of teachers be passive readers if they so prefer, and feel free not to contribute to the accumulation. Let not the prosecution of it be preached as an imperative duty or imposed by regulation on those to whom it proves an exterminating bore. . . . I cannot too strongly agree with my colleague, Professor Münsterberg, when he says that the teacher's attitude toward the child, being concrete and ethical, is positively opposed to the psy-

chological observer's, which is abstract and analytic (*Talks to Teachers and Students*. New York: Holt, 1899, pp. 12–13).

27   For a discussion of methods used in child study, see Luckey, George W. A. A brief survey of child study. *North Western Journal of Education*, 1896, 7, 2–8; Siegel, A. W., & White, S. H. The child study movement: Early growth and development of the symbolized child. In H. W. Reese & L. Lipsitt (Eds.), *Advances in Child Development and Behavior* (Vol. 17). New York: Academic Press, 1982, pp. 233–285.

28   Wolfe, The state societies, p. 45; Wiltse, Sara E. A preliminary sketch of the history of child study in America. *Pedagogical Seminary*, 1895, 3, 185–212. See pages 206–208 for Wolfe's description of his child study courses at the University of Nebraska.

29   Frances Evelyn Duncombe conducted the study on children's ideas about Santa Claus as part of a child study class she took from Wolfe. She published a detailed description of her research methods and data in the *North Western Journal of Education*, 1896, 7, 37–42. The account was so detailed that a direct replication of the study was performed on a comparable sample of Lincoln schoolchildren in 1977. See Benjamin, Ludy T., Jr., Langley, Jacqueline F., & Hall, Rosalie J. Santa, now and then. *Psychology Today*, December 1979, pp. 36–44.

30   Wolfe, Harry K. Simple observations and experiments. *North Western Journal of Education*, 1896, 7, 36–37.

31   Wolfe, Harry K. *The practical value of child study*. Unpublished lecture. Wolfe Papers, UNA.

32   Wolfe, Harry K. *The measure of men*. Unpublished lecture, May 11, 1918, p. 5. WFP.

33   Wolfe, Harry K. Some effects of size on judgments of weight. *Psychological Review*, 1898, 5, 27.

34   Ibid., p. 26.

35   Wolfe, Harry K. *Sense defects of school children*. 8 pp.; *Defects in hearing*. 6 pp. Unpublished lectures. WFP.

36   See, for example, Wolfe's regular column, "The Study of Children," in the *North Western Journal of Education*.

37   Wolfe, The state societies, p. 45.

38   Ibid., p. 46.

39   Ibid., p. 47.

40   Ibid., p. 47.

41   Editorial, *North Western Journal of Education*, 1896, 7, 1. Luckey and

Wolfe were coeditors of this issue devoted solely to child study.

42   Manley, Robert N. *Centennial History of the University of Nebraska, I: Frontier University, 1869–1919*. Lincoln: University of Nebraska Press, 1969. See pp. 171–173, quote on p. 172.

43   Münsterberg, Hugo. School reform. *Atlantic Monthly*, 1900, *85*, 656–669; Hall, G. Stanley. The case of the public schools. *Atlantic Monthly*, 1896, *77*, 403–413.

44   See, for example, Cavallo, D. *Muscles and Morals*. Philadelphia: University of Pennsylvania Press, 1981; Macleod, D. I. *Building Character in the American Boy*. Madison: University of Wisconsin Press, 1983.

45   Hall, G. Stanley. *Youth: Its Education, Regimen, and Hygiene*. New York: Appleton, 1906.

46   Hall, G. Stanley. *Adolescence: Its Psychology and Its Relations to Physiology, Anthropology, Sociology, Sex, Crime, Religion, and Education* (Vols. 1 & 2). New York: Appleton, 1904; Ross, *G. Stanley Hall*, p. 325.

47   Frederick Kuhlmann earned his B.A. degree at the University of Nebraska in 1899, getting his initial exposure to psychology from Wolfe. His career in mental testing is described briefly in the Appendix of this book.

48   Anderson, John E. Child development: An historical perspective. *Child Development*, 1956, *27*, 181–196.

49   Belden, E. *A history of the child study movement in the United States, 1870–1920, with special reference to its scientific and educational background*. Unpublished doctoral dissertation, University of California, Berkeley, 1965, p. 2.

50   This taxonomy of child study goals is taken from Siegel & White, The child study movement.

51   Wolfe, *The theory of child study*, p. 20. Wolfe Papers, UNA.

Chapter 5: Politics in the Academy

Three sources were especially important for this chapter: (1) interviews with Isabel Wolfe Hemenway, Katharine A. Wolfe, and Harry Kirke Wolfe II; (2) the Wolfe Family Papers (WFP); and (3) the Walter B. Pillsbury Papers, which are part of the Michigan Historical Collections, Bentley Historical Library, University of Michigan, Ann Arbor.

1   Letter from H. K. Wolfe to Edward B. Titchener, August 5, 1895. Titchener Papers, Cornell University Library, Ithaca, NY.

2 Letter from H. K. Wolfe to Walter Pillsbury, November 2, 1895. Pillsbury Papers.

3 Ibid., January 14, 1896, and March 27, 1896. Pillsbury Papers.

4 Ibid., April 15, 1896. Pillsbury Papers.

5 Ibid.

6 Ibid.

7 Ibid., May 3, 1896. Pillsbury Papers.

8 Ibid.

9 Copy of statement signed by seventy-nine students and presented to Chancellor MacLean. Though undated, it was certainly written during the 1895–96 academic year. WFP.

10 His letter is made public. *Omaha World Herald,* June 15, 1897, p. 3.

11 Ibid.

12 Dr. Wolfe is removed. *Hesperian,* April 30, 1897, p. 7. Enrollment at the University of Nebraska for the 1896–97 academic year was officially 1,653.

13 Ibid.

14 Ibid. Note that the religious issue is raised in this report.

15 Letter from H. K. Wolfe to University of Nebraska Board of Regents, June 10, 1897. Board of Regents Papers, UNA.

16 Letter from H. K. Wolfe to Walter Pillsbury, May 8, 1897. Pillsbury Papers.

17 Letter from Jacob V. Wolfe to University of Nebraska Board of Regents, June 10, 1897. Board of Regents Papers, UNA.

18 Wolfe to Nebraska Board of Regents, June 10, 1897. Board of Regents Papers, UNA.

19 Manley, Robert N. *Centennial History of the University of Nebraska, I: Frontier University, 1869–1919.* Lincoln: University of Nebraska Press, 1969.

20 Hudson H. Nicholson, letter addressed "To Whom It May Concern." This letter was part of a public file at the University of Nebraska. Wolfe copied the letter by hand in the spring or summer of 1896. However, when the file was checked again in the summer of 1897, that letter and Wolfe's response to it had disappeared. Neither letter exists today in the University of Nebraska–Lincoln Archives, but copies of both letters are in the Wolfe Family Papers.

21 Letter from H. K. Wolfe to Chancellor George MacLean, Spring 1896. Original disappeared (see previous note). Copy in WFP.

22 *Omaha World Herald,* June 15, 1897; Prof. Wolfe talks. *Lincoln Evening Post,* June 15, 1897, p. 1.

23 Letter from H. K. Wolfe to regents, June 10, 1897. Board of Regents Papers, UNA.

24   Ibid. According to the records of Phi Beta Kappa, the University of Nebraska chapter was officially established in 1895. It is ironic that both of Wolfe's daughters, Isabel and Katharine, graduated Phi Beta Kappa from the University of Nebraska. Wolfe's son, Harry, who graduated from the University of Washington in architecture, was not eligible because he was not an arts and sciences major.

25   Wolfe to Pillsbury, May 8, 1897. Pillsbury Papers.

26   Fusionists, sometimes called the Bryancratic party, were the Populists who joined ranks with the Democrats, supporting William Jennings Bryan for president. See Manley, *Centennial History*, pp. 119–120.

27   Dr. Wolfe will suffer. *Lincoln Evening Post*, June 19, 1897, p. 1.

28   See, for example, *Lincoln Evening Post*, June 15, 1897; *Omaha World Herald*, June 15, 1897.

29   Prof. Wolfe talks, p. 1.

30   Cannot remain silent. *Lincoln Evening Post*, June 16, 1897, p. 3.

31   Dr. Wolfe will suffer. *Lincoln Evening Post*, June 19, 1897, p. 1.

32   Ibid.

33   Giving the reason. *Lincoln Evening Post*, June 19, 1897, p. 2.

34   Queer press comment. *Lincoln Evening Post*, December 8, 1897, p. 1.

35   See, for example, editorial by J. H. Miller, *North Western Journal of Education*, 1897, 7, 321.

36   Iowa aflame over row at University. Newspaper clipping (newspaper not identified). Published around May 24, 1903. WFP. The article describes MacLean's early troubles as the president of the University of Iowa and reports on some of his difficulties while he was chancellor of the University of Nebraska.

37   For information on George Edwin MacLean (1850–1938), see Pound, Louise. MacLean, George Edwin. In *Dictionary of American Biography* (Vol. 22). New York: Scribner's, 1958, pp. 419–420; Gerber, John C. *A Pictorial History of the University of Iowa*. Iowa City: University of Iowa Press, 1988, pp. 55–57; Johnson, Ellen E. *A History of the State University of Iowa: The administration of President MacLean*. Unpublished master's thesis, University of Iowa, Iowa City, 1946.

38   Wolfe, Harry K. Some effects of size on judgments of weight. *Psychological Review*, 1898, 5, 25–54; idem, Some judgments on the size of familiar objects. *American Journal of Psychology*, 1898, 9, 137–166.

39   Chudacoff, Howard P. Where rolls the dark Missouri down. *Ne-*

braska History, 1971, *52*, 1–30.

40 Wenger, Robert E. The Anti-Saloon League in Nebraska politics, 1898–1910. *Nebraska History,* 1971, *52*, 267–292.

41 As a student in Germany, Wolfe skipped meals to buy the prints and statues that appealed to him, returning—much thinner—to the United States with his art treasures.

42 The difference between Omaha and South Omaha. *Omaha World Herald,* February 9, 1901, p. 1.

43 Isabel Wolfe Hemenway, interview with author, 1981.

44 The three NYU professors resigned from the Department of Pedagogy "owing to continued dissatisfaction with the administration of the Department." See Notes and news, *Psychological Review,* 1901, *8*, 336.

45 Letters from James Canfield (July 26, 1901) and Benjamin Andrews (July 17, 1901) to Henry MacCracken. WFP; Notes and news. *Psychological Review,* 1901, *8*, 447.

46 Letter from George M. Stratton to George H. Howison, July 26, 1902. Howison Papers, Bancroft Library, University of California–Berkeley. Stratton wrote: "My own doubt is about his [Wolfe's] age (L. says 40–45 yrs) and the fact that he seems to have produced so little since his Leipzig *Arbeit* in 1886. That piece of work was good, however. I have never seen him."

47 Letter from Charles Bessey to Frank P. Graves, May 6, 1902. WFP.

48 South Omaha approved funding for a new high school building in 1903, two years after Wolfe's departure from the superintendent's job.

49 Wolfe, H. K. Pictures in the school room. *North Western Monthly,* 1898, *8*, 380. See also Wolfe, H. K. Comenius. *North Western Journal of Education,* 1892, *2*, 226–233.

50 In the Lincoln Schools. *Lincoln State Journal,* January 3, 1904, p. 2. It was while he was at Lincoln High School that Wolfe met a student who would eventually choose a career in psychology. A teacher at the school brought Wolfe a paper on philosophy, supposedly authored by a senior student. The teacher believed it was plagiarized but could not locate the source. Wolfe read the paper and then invited the student to meet with him. After talking briefly with the student, Wolfe was convinced that the ideas were indeed those of the young man. The student's name was Edwin R. Guthrie, and he would become one of America's most eminent psychologists (see the Appendix). Guthrie later studied with Wolfe at the University of Nebraska. See Sheffield, Fred D.

Edwin Ray Guthrie: 1886–1959. *American Journal of Psychology,* 1959, 72, 642–650.

51 Interview with Katharine Alice Wolfe and Isabel Wolfe Hemenway. Sidney was born May 8, 1892, and died October 21, 1893. Katharine and Harry were born May 16, 1904, and January 23, 1908 respectively.

52 Will take time to elect a successor. *Omaha World Herald,* exact date unknown (Spring 1904).

53 Letter from O. J. Craig to H. K. Wolfe, December 8, 1904. WFP.

54 Letter from Charles E. Bessey to H. K. Wolfe, December 24, 1904. WFP.

55 Program of the Cascade County Teacher's Institute. Great Falls, Montana, August 30—September 1, 1905. WFP.

56 Letter from George W. A. Luckey to E. Benjamin Andrews, September 12, 1905. Wolfe Papers, UNA; Letter from E. Benjamin Andrews to H. K. Wolfe, October 17, 1905. Wolfe Papers, UNA. In their book *Educational Psychology: Principles and Applications* (2 nd ed.), published by Little Brown and Company in 1986, John A. Glover and Roger H. Bruning list H. K. Wolfe as the first person to hold the title of Professor of Educational Psychology, a title they say he held as early as 1895. However, I can find no records that indicate he held that title before 1906.

57 Letter from H. K. Wolfe to E. Benjamin Andrews, October 21, 1905. Wolfe Papers, UNA.

58 Sendoff for Dr. Wolfe. *Missoula Standard,* February 2, 1906, p. 2.

59 A blot wiped out. *Omaha World Herald,* November 25, 1905, p. 6. See also *Nebraska Teacher,* November 1905, p. 230.

60 Wolfe, H. K. The new psychology in undergraduate work. *Psychological Review,* 1895, 2, 382–387; French, F. C. The place of experimental psychology in the undergraduate course. *Psychological Review,* 1898, 3, 510–512.

61 On his return to Nebraska in 1906, Wolfe was elected president of the University of Nebraska Alumni Association. During that year Wolfe also assumed the editorship of the *University Journal.* Because of the growing interest in local alumni clubs, a section of the *Journal* was devoted to news about the activities of these clubs. see Reeder, Ralph L. History of Nebraska's Alumni Association. *Nebraska Alumnus,* January 1940, pp. 2–7.

62 Miner, Burt G. The changing attitude of American universities toward psychology. *Science,* 1904, 20, 299–307.

63 See 1904–5 correspondence of Thaddeus Lincoln Bolton. Board of Regents Papers, UNA.

64 Winifred Hyde left Nebraska in 1928 to marry Edwin M. Dodd, Jr., a professor of law at Nebraska, who had accepted a position at Harvard University. They were both killed in an automobile accident in Portsmouth, New Hampshire, on November 4, 1951.

Chapter 6: Patriotism on Trial

This chapter, like others, uses information from interviews with Isabel Wolfe Hemenway, Katharine A. Wolfe, and Harry Kirke Wolfe II. It also draws substantially from the Nebraska State Council of Defense records, 1917–18, which are housed in the manuscript collections of the Nebraska State Historical Society, Lincoln, Nebraska. In the notes that follow, references to that collection are designated "Defense Council Records." Two other sources were especially important, both authored by the historian Robert N. Manley. One is his master's thesis on the Nebraska State Council of Defense, the other is his *Centennial History of the University of Nebraska*. Both are referenced fully in the notes that follow.

1 Olson, James C. *History of Nebraska* (2nd ed.). Lincoln: University of Nebraska Press, 1966, chapter 21: Nebraska and World War I.

2 Nebraska editors discuss facts in regents' hearing. *Lincoln Daily Star*, June 17, 1918, p. 2. (cites *Aurora Republican*).

3 Luebke, Frederick C. The German-American Alliance in Nebraska, 1910–1917. *Nebraska History*, 1968, 49, 165–187.

4 Niebuhr, Reinhold. The failure of German-Americanism. *Atlantic Monthly*, 1916, 118, 13–18. For an example of the diatribes against German-Americans, see Skaggs, W. H. *German Conspiracies in America*. London: Fisher, Unwin, 1915.

5 Hale, Matthew, Jr. *Human Science and Social Order: Hugo Münsterberg and the Origins of Applied Psychology*. Philadelphia: Temple University Press, 1980.

6 Quoted in Luebke, Frederick C. *Bonds of Loyalty: German-Americans and World War I*. Dekalb, IL: Northern Illinois University Press, 1974. p. 90.

7 Keller, Phyllis. *States of Belonging: German-American Intellectuals and the First World War*. Cambridge: Harvard University Press, 1979. Münsterberg's final years were unhappy ones; his love for Germany and America created an impossible situation for one who felt so passionately and believed so firmly. He died on December 16, 1916, at the age of fifty-three, while lecturing to a

class at Radcliffe College. Thus he was spared, at least, seeing the United States declare war on Germany.

8   Wittke, Carl. *German-Americans and the World War*. Columbus: Ohio State Archeological and Historical Society, 1936.

9   Charles Bryan's loss was in part due to his brother's resignation as Wilson's secretary of state in 1915. The elder Bryan resigned because of Wilson's fading neutrality, a decision that cost W. J. Bryan considerable popularity in Nebraska, particularly once the United States entered the war.

10   Manley, Robert N. *Centennial History of the University of Nebraska, I: Frontier University, 1869–1919*. Lincoln: University of Nebraska Press, 1969, pp. 213–214. See also, Manley, R. N. *The Nebraska State Council of Defense: Loyalty programs and policies during World War I*. Unpublished master's thesis, University of Nebraska, Lincoln, 1959.

11   Manley, *Centennial History*, p. 212.

12   Ibid., p. 214. All will support the war. *Nebraska State Journal*, April 10, 1917, p. 1.

13   Carlson, Robert E. Professor Fred Fling: His career and conflicts at Nebraska University. *Nebraska History*, 1981, *62*, 481–496. Carlson is one of several sources stating that Fling was used as one of the characters in Willa Cather's Pulitzer Prize–winning novel *One of Ours* (1922).

14   Peterson, Horace C., & Fite, Gilbert C. *Opponents of War, 1917–1918*. Madison: University of Wisconsin Press, 1957, pp. 194, 195.

15   Wittke, *German-Americans and the World War*; Johnson, Niel M. The Missouri Synod Lutherans and the war against the German language. *Nebraska History*, 1975, *56*, 137–144; Rodgers, Jack W. The foreign language issue in Nebraska, 1918–1923. *Nebraska History*, 1958, *39*, 1–22. See also the article by Sarka B. Hrbkova, a member of the Nebraska State Council of Defense, calling for a repeal of the Siman Language Law: Bunk in Americanization, *Forum*, 1920, *63*, 428–439.

16   Peterson & Fite, *Opponents of War*, p. 102.

17   Manley, *Centennial History*, p. 216.

18   Letter from the Council to University of Nebraska Board of Regents, April 19, 1918. Defense Council Records.

19   See Peterson & Fite, *Opponents of War*, for coverage of faculty dismissals in many colleges and universities.

20   Tolman, Edward C. Autobiography. In E. G. Boring, H. S. Langfeld, H. Werner, & R. M. Yerkes (Eds.), *A History of Psychology in Autobiography* (Vol. 4). Worcester, MA: Clark University

Press, 1952, pp. 323–340. Late in his career, Tolman successfully led a fight against a required loyalty oath for the state of California. He was principally responsible for writing the brief that went to the California Supreme Court.

21   Cattell's dismissal from Columbia was a long time in the making. He was disliked by Columbia's president, Nicholas Murray Butler, and by several of the trustees, and attempts to fire him had been made before. The letter to Congress offered Butler and the trustees the opportunity they had been waiting for. For a description of Cattell's case, see Gruber, Carol S. Academic freedom at Columbia University, 1917–1918: The case of James McKeen Cattell. *AAUP Bulletin, 1972, 58,* 297–305; Gruber, C. S. *Mars and Minerva: World War I and the Uses of Higher Learning in America.* Baton Rouge: Louisiana State University Press, 1975; Summerscales, William. *Affirmation and Dissent: Columbia's Response to the Crisis of World War I.* New York: Teachers College Press, 1970.

22   Council requests house-cleaning at state university. *Lincoln Daily Star,* April 19, 1918, pp. 1, 4; Plenty to investigate. *Lincoln Daily Star,* April 23, 1918, p. 6.

23   Letter from the regents to Council of Defense, April 25, 1918. Defense Council Records.

24   Council meets to reply to regents. *Lincoln Daily Star,* April 26, 1918, p. 10.

25   Minutes of May 17, 1918, meeting, p. 1. Defense Council Records.

26   Ibid.

27   Ibid., p. 7.

28   12 professors to be heard Tuesday. *Omaha Daily News,* May 26, 1918, p. 2C; Regents decide on immediate hearing. *Omaha Morning World Herald,* May 26, 1918, pp. 1, 2.

29   Regents' board hearing charges of state council. *Lincoln Daily Star,* May 28, 1918, pp. 1, 4; 12 university men on trial. *Omaha Evening Bee,* May 28, 1918, pp. 1, 2.

30   Regents' board hearing charges of state council, p. 4.

31   Ibid; University hearing on loyalty broadened. *Omaha Morning World Herald,* May 29, 1918, pp. 1, 2.

32   Prof. Wolfe, not on council list, before regents. *Lincoln Daily Star,* May 29, 1918, pp. 1, 4. Letter to the Council from "A Taxpayer," not dated. Defense Council Records. For many Americans who, like Wolfe, were educated in Germany, the widespread denigration of *everything* German created a painful conflict. As G. Stanley Hall described it, "my soul [felt] almost

torn in two between a sense of loyalty to and admiration of civic and cultural Germany, from whom we have yet so much to learn, and German militarism." See Hall's foreword in George Blakeslee (Ed.), *Problems and Lessons of the War*. New York: Knickerbocker Press, 1916, pp. ix–xxiv.

33   Testimony of H. K. Wolfe, May 29, 1918, 18 pp. Defense Council Records. The quotations in the paragraphs that follow are also from this source.

34   Prof. Wolfe not on council list. For a more negative report, see Persinger interview introduced in quiz. *Omaha Morning World Herald*, May 30, 1918, pp. 1, 2.

35   Drop two charges in regents' hearings. *Omaha Morning World Herald*, June 1, 1918, pp. 1, 16.

36   Avery says war record of university is good. *Omaha Sunday World Herald*, June 2, 1918, pp. 1, 4; Chancellor Avery says few faculty members passive. *Lincoln Daily Star*, June 2, 1918, pp. 1, 4; University loyal, says chancellor. *Omaha Daily News*, June 2, 1918, pp. 1, 2.

37   Minutes of May 17, 1918, meeting. Defense Council Records; Regents wait on report of hearing. *Lincoln Daily Star*, June 12, 1918, pp. 1, 8; Witnesses say professors are loyal to America. *Omaha Morning World Herald*, May 29, 1918, pp. 1, 2.

38   Regents wait on report of hearing, pp. 1, 8.

39   Gurley asks for the dismissal of eight professors. *Lincoln Daily Star*, June 11, 1918, pp. 1, 4.

40   Dismiss eight faculty members Gurley demands. *Omaha Evening Bee*, June 11, 1918, p. 1; Regents wait on report of hearing. *Omaha Evening Bee*, June 12, 1918, pp. 1, 8; Ask clean bill for 8 professors. *Omaha Daily News*, June 11, 1918, p. 3; Gurley asks for the dismissal of eight professors, pp. 1, 4.

41   Regents request resignations of three teachers. *Lincoln Daily Star*, June 19, 1918, pp. 1, 4; Manley, *Centennial History*, p. 224.

42   Manley, *Centennial History*, p. 224 (based on Manley's interview with Bertha Luckey).

43   Decree of Board Persinger Hopt, Luckey must go. *Omaha Evening Bee*, June 19, 1918, p. 3; Regents demand Hopt, Persinger, Luckey resign. *Omaha Morning World Herald*, June 19, 1918, p. 1. See also *Lincoln Daily Star*, June 19, 1918.

44   Peregrinus, Censor. A university in a university court. *Nation*, 1918, *106*, 732–734. Jurisconsultus. Trial of the Nebraska professors. *Educational Review*, 1918, *56*, 415–423.

45   Neville says he will run again. *Lincoln Daily Star*, June 7, 1918, p. 1.

46 Manley, *Centennial History*, p. 225. See also *Omaha Daily News, Lincoln Daily Star,* and *Omaha Sunday World Herald* for June 2, 1918.

47 Peregrinus, A university in a university court, p. 732.

48 Peterson & Fite, *Opponents of War.*

49 Gruber, *Mars and Minerva,* pp. 163, 169. For a description of the federal government's intervention in education during World War I, see Todd, Lewis P. *Wartime Relations of the Federal Government and the Public Schools, 1917–1918.* New York: Teachers College Press, 1945.

50 G.W.A. Luckey wrote to Wolfe on July 29, 1918: "I am glad however that the hysteria of the board took me rather than you or Professor Caldwell, both equally innocent but of greater worth to the University. . . . I did not expect such inhuman treatment from the board." The letter was never mailed because Luckey learned of Wolfe's death the next day. The letter was later sent to Katharine B. Wolfe. WFP.

51 Reference to letter from Wolfe to Ned Culbertson Abbott is in an unpublished manuscript by Abbott. WFP.

52 These two items are from the *Nebraska State Journal* (Lincoln). Exact dates are unknown, but both are believed to have been published in August 1918. The first is signed "Bix," the second is anonymous.

53 Wolfe, H. K. Personality and education. *Mid-West Quarterly,* 1918, *5,* 271–272.

54 Katharine Brandt Wolfe used the name Katharine H. K. Wolfe after the death of her husband. She lived the remainder of her long life in Seattle. She died in 1960 at the age of ninety-four.

55 Professors score in loyalty hearing. *Omaha Morning World Herald,* June 6, 1918, pp. 1, 3.

56 Alexander, Hartley B. Harry Kirke Wolfe: 1858–1918. *Science,* 1918, *48,* 312–313. See also *Nebraska State Journal* (Lincoln), August 4, 1918.

57 Alexander, H. B. The Nebraska decision. *Nation,* 1918, *107,* 14–15. Part of Alexander's plan for the "new" professor was a salary increase. "This new conception of duties will profoundly affect the status of the profession of college teaching—and almost certainly to its eventual benefit. The professor will come to be looked upon not as a pensioner of society, but as a citizen; his position will no longer be regarded as a sinecure for the socially incompetent, but as demanding abilities and as attended by risks, just as business and politics have their risks. No doubt

this will affect the apparent attractiveness of the teaching profession, to which security of tenure has certainly contributed. But eventually this will be compensated by increase in the direct returns, in the salaries paid." It is possible that Alexander wrote this article with tongue firmly implanted in cheek. But if he did so, that intent is well disguised.

Chapter 7: A Teacher Is Forever

1   A memorial. *Omaha World Herald*, undated, but likely published between August and November, 1918. WFP.

2   Laurence Fossler had been an undergraduate student with Wolfe, finishing a year behind him in the Class of 1881. Fossler's family farmed near the Wolfes, and he and Wolfe had played together as boys. Their close friendship continued throughout their lives. Fossler was questioned by the State Council of Defense in 1918 about his opposition to the elimination of German language instruction in the public schools; however, he was never formally charged.

3   Printed letter sent to Palladians and former Palladians, January 1920. It was signed by the seven members of the Wolfe Fellowship Committee. Wolfe Papers, UNA. See also In memory of Doctor Wolfe. *Nebraska State Journal*, (Lincoln), May 25, 1919, p. 6.

4   Letter from T.F.A. Williams to "Fellow Palladians," dated January 10, 1930. WFP.

5   See, for example, Bartlett, Neil R., Reed, J. D., & Duvoisin, G. Estimations of distance on polar coordinate plots as a function of the scale used. *Journal of General Psychology*, 1949, *41*, 47–65.

6   Wolfe, H. K. The new psychology in undergraduate work. *Psychological Review*, 1895, *2*, 382–387.

7   Bentley, Autobiography. In Carl Murchison (Ed.), *A History of Psychology in Autobiography* (Vol. 3). Worcester, MA: Clark University Press, 1936, pp. 53–67.

8   *Wolfe, H. K. The psychology of research.* Unpublished lecture. Wolfe Papers, UNA.

9   Remarks by Hartley B. Alexander at the funeral service for Wolfe, August 3, 1918. WFP.

10 Johnson, Alvin. *Pioneers Progress.* Lincoln: University of Nebraska Press, 1960, p. 114.

11 Another name for the "new" psychology in the latter part of the nineteenth century was "physiological psychology." That label

was part of the title used by Wundt in his most important work, *Principles of Physiological Psychology,* first published in 1873–74, and was also used by Yale University's George Trumbull Ladd, whose *Elements of Physiological Psychology,* published in 1887, marked the first American text in the new psychology. Wolfe used Ladd's text in his initial year of teaching at Nebraska.

Like Alvin Johnson, many students today are often dismayed by the extensive coverage of the biological and biochemical bases of behavior that is a part of the college introductory psychology course.

12 From the collection of student reminiscences prepared by Ned C. Abbott for presentation at the December 8, 1918, Wolfe Memorial Service at the University of Nebraska, pp. 1–8. WFP.

13 Ibid., p. 6.

14 Letter from H. K. Wolfe to Walter Pillsbury, May 3, 1896. Pillsbury Papers, Michigan Historical Collections, Bentley Historical Library, University of Michigan, Ann Arbor.

15 Boring, Mollie E., & Boring, Edwin G. Masters and pupils among the American psychologists. *American Journal of Psychology,* 1949, *61,* 527–534.

16 Hinman, Edgar L. Harry Kirke Wolfe (1858–1918). In D. Malone (Ed.), *Dictionary of American Biography* (Vol. 10). New York: Scribners, 1936, pp. 450–451.

17 Wolfe, H. K. Some questions in professional ethics. *Education,* 1899, *19,* 466.

18 Wolfe, H. K., *Philosophy and ethics,* p. 2. Unpublished lecture. Wolfe Papers, UNA.

19 Ibid., p. 27.

20 Letter from Isabel Wolfe Hemenway to L. T. Benjamin, Jr., January 1982.

21 Will take time to elect a successor. *Omaha World Herald,* exact date unknown (Spring 1904); Letter from Charles E. Bessey to Frank P. Graves (President, University of Washington), May 5, 1902. WFP.

22 Letter from Howard W. Caldwell addressed "To Whom it May Concern," April 22, 1901. WFP.

23 Letter from H. K. Wolfe to Walter Pillsbury, May 8, 1897. Pillsbury Papers. Cora L. Friedline was a 1913 graduate of the University of Nebraska and one of Wolfe's laboratory assistants. She did her graduate work at Cornell University, earning her Ph.D. in psychology with Titchener in 1918. She died in 1975, leaving two hundred thousand dollars to the University of Ne-

braska in honor of Wolfe. She noted, "[Wolfe was] the most inspiring professor I ever had and by far the most important factor in guiding my career." See the Appendix for additional information on Friedline.

24 Wolfe lacked the inflated ego necessary to achieve the kinds of accomplishments that distinguished the careers of Hall and Cattell. Cattell seemed to know from his earliest days in Wundt's laboratory that he was going to be an important psychologist. He wrote to his parents about how Wundt appreciated his "phenomenal genius." And in an 1885 letter, written after his first paper was published and while still a graduate student, he told his parents, "A paper like this gives me a very secure place in the scientific world, makes me equal with any American living." See Sokal, Michael M., *An Education in Psychology: James McKeen Cattell's Journal and Letters from Germany and England, 1880–1888*. Cambridge, MA: MIT Press, 1981, p. 192.

25 Letter from H. K. Wolfe to Katharine B. Wolfe, December 29, 1916, WFP. A portion of the letter reads: "Have just returned from evening meeting of the Association. I am now a member (except the payment of dues) of the Am. Psy. Association. It has been a day worth while. If you all keep well I shall be glad I came. I needed this experience in any business. I have already met many of the men, the Bentleys, Pillsbury, Bolton, Hollingworth and his wife, Bean, all these formerly of Nebraska. I saw Cattell for a few minutes. He was unusually cordial."

26 Alexander, Hartley B. Harry Kirke Wolfe (1858–1918). *Science*, 1918, *48*, 312–313.

27 Adams, Henry B. *The Education of Henry Adams*. Boston: Houghton Mifflin, 1961, p. 300. Originally published in 1907.

Appendix

1 McCready, Eric S. The Nebraska State Capitol: Its design, background, and influence. *Nebraska History*, 1974, *55*, 325–461.

2 Pound, Louise. Hartley Alexander as an undergraduate. *Prairie Schooner*, 1948, *22*, 372–377; *Scripps College Bulletin*, 1940. Special issue in memory of H. B. Alexander.

3 Arnold, Henry J. *National Cyclopedia of American Biography*, 1965, *48*, 377–378.

4 Benson, Charles E. *National Cyclopedia of American Biography*, 1968, *50*, 363–364.

5   Dallenbach, Karl M. Madison Bentley: 1870–1955. *American Journal of Psychology,* 1956, *69,* 169–193; Bentley, M. Autobiography. In Carl Murchison (Ed.), *A History of Psychology in Autobiography* (Vol. 3). Worcester, MA: Clark University Press, 1936, pp. 53–67.

6   Letter from Horace B. English to H. K. Wolfe, February 2, 1912. WFP.

7   Transcript of a May 3, 1966, lecture by Cora L. Friedline to the History and Systems of Psychology class at Randolph-Macon College for Women. Copy in Friedline Papers, Archives of the History of American Psychology, University of Akron, Ohio.

8   Letter from Cora L. Friedline to Isabel Wolfe Hemenway, March 31, 1968. WFP.

9   Sheffield, Fred D. Edwin Ray Guthrie: 1886–1959. *American Journal of Psychology,* 1959, *72,* 642–650; American Psychological Foundation Gold Medal Award. *American Psychologist,* 1958, *13,* 739–740.

10   Jenkins, Thomas N. *National Cyclopedia of American Biography,* 1969, *51,* 419.

11   Dallenbach, Karl M. Frederick Kuhlmann: 1876–1941. *American Journal of Psychology,* 1941, *54,* 446–447.

12   Lund, Frederick H. *National Cyclopedia of American Biography,* 1970, *52,* 273–274; Leaders in education, xiii: Dr. Frederick H. Lund. *Education,* 1959, *79,* 317–318.

13   Dallenbach, Karl M. Walter Bowers Pillsbury: 1872–1960. *American Journal of Psychology,* 1961, *74,* 165–176; Pillsbury, W. B. Autobiography. In Carl Murchison (Ed.), *A History of Psychology in Autobiography* (Vol. 2). Worcester, MA: Clark University Press, 1932, pp. 265–295; Miles, Walter R. Walter Bowers Pillsbury: 1872–1960. *National Academy of Sciences Biographical Memoirs,* 1964, *37,* 267–291; Raphelson, Alfred C. Psychology at Michigan: The Pillsbury years. *Journal of the History of the Behavioral Sciences,* 1980, *16,* 301–312.

14   Fernberger, Samuel W. Further statistics of the American Psychological Association. *Psychological Bulletin,* 1921, *18,* 569–572; Fernberger, S. W. Statistical analyses of the members and associates of the American Psychological Association, Inc. *Psychological Review,* 1928, *35,* 447–465.

15   Poffenberger, Albert T. Harry Levi Hollingworth: 1880–1956. *American Journal of Psychology,* 1957, *70,* 136–140.

16   Benjamin, Ludy T., Jr. The pioneering work of Leta Hollingworth in the psychology of women. *Nebraska History,* 1975, *56,*

493–505; Hollingworth, Harry L. *Leta Stetter Hollingworth: A Biography*. Lincoln: University of Nebraska Press, 1943 (reprinted 1990 by Anker Publishing Co., Bolton, MA); Shields, Stephanie A. Ms. Pilgrim's progress: The contributions of Leta Stetter Hollingworth to the psychology of women. *American Psychologist*, 1975, *30*, 852–857; Benjamin, L. T., Jr., & Shields, S. A. Leta Stetter Hollingworth. In Agnes N. O'Connell & Nancy F. Russo (Eds.), *Women in Psychology*. New York: Greenwood Press, 1990.

17 Michael, William B., Comrey, Andrew L., & Fruchter, Benjamin. J. P. Guilford: Psychologist and teacher. *Psychological Bulletin*, 1963, *60*, 1–34; Comrey, A. L., Michael, W. B., & Fruchter, B. J. P. Guilford (1897–1987). *American Psychologist*, 1988, *43*, 1086–1087; Guilford, J. P. Autobiography. In Edwin G. Boring & Gardner Lindzey (Eds.), *A History of Psychology in Autobiography* (Vol. 5). New York: Appleton-Century-Crofts, 1967, pp. 167–191.

18 Letter from Joseph McVicker Hunt to L. T. Benjamin, Jr., September 29, 1987.

19 Hunt, Joseph McV. A professional odyssey. In Theophile S. Krawiec (Ed.), *The Psychologists* (Vol. 2). New York: Oxford University Press, 1974.

20 Benjamin, L. T., Jr., & Bertelson, Amy D. The early Nebraska psychology laboratory, 1889–1930: Nursery for presidents of the American Psychological Association. *Journal of the History of the Behavioral Sciences*, 1975, *11*, 142–148.

Bibliography of Harry Kirke Wolfe

1   Untersuchungen über das Tongedächtniss. [Studies on the memory for tones.] *Philosophische Studien*, 1886, *3*, 534–571.
2   On the color-vocabulary of children. *University Studies* (Nebraska), 1890, *1*, 205–234.
3   Psychology at the University of Nebraska. *American Journal of Psychology*, 1890, *3*:, 276–277.
4   Observations on the study of children. *Education*, 1890, *11*, 201–207.
5   Comenius. *North Western Journal of Education*, 1892, *2*, 226–233.
6   Notes on educational method. *Educational Review*, 1892, *4*, 27–33.
7   Psychology as a fad. *North Western Journal of Education*, 1893, *4*, 16.
8   The normal school question. *North Western Journal of Education*, 1894, *4*, 188–189.
9   Report of the Educational Council of the Nebraska State Teachers Association. *North Western Journal of Education*, 1894, *4*, 249.
10 The study of children. *North Western Journal of Education*, 1894, *5*, 54–55.
11 The study of children. *North Western Journal of Education*, 1894, *5*, 82–83.
12 The study of children. *North Western Journal of Education*, 1894, *5*, 116–117.
13 The new psychology in undergraduate work. *Psychological Review*, 1895, *2*, 382–387.
14 The study of children. *North Western Journal of Education*, 1895, *5*, 177–178.
15 Pedagogy in the University of Nebraska. *North Western Journal of Education*, 1895, *5*, 269–270.

16 The study of children: An introduction. *North Western Journal of Education*, 1895, *6*, 76.

17 The study of children: The child at birth. *North Western Journal of Education*, 1895, *6*, 97–98.

18 The study of children: The first year of life. *North Western Journal of Education*, 1895, *6*, 130–131.

19 The study of children: The second year of life. *North Western Journal of Education*, 1895, *6*, 156–157.

20 The study of children: The growth of the body. *North Western Journal of Education*, 1896, *6*, 192–193.

21 The study of children: Suggestive experiments. *North Western Journal of Education*, 1896, *6*, 206–207.

22 The study of children: The child at school age. *North Western Journal of Education*, 1896, *6*, 238–240.

23 The study of children: The beginnings of speech. *North Western Journal of Education*, 1896, *6*, 267–269.

24 The study of children: The beginnings of intellect. *North Western Journal of Education*, 1896, *6*, 289–291.

25 The study of children: Imagination and emotion. *North Western Journal of Education*, 1896, *6*, 319–320.

26 Historical sketch of child study. *North Western Journal of Education*, 1896, *7*, 9–12.

27 Common defects of children. *North Western Journal of Education*, 1896, *7*, 22–23.

28 Simple observations and experiments. *North Western Journal of Education*, 1896, *7*, 36–37.

29 The state societies for child study. *North Western Journal of Education*, 1896, *7*, 42–46.

30 Some defects of school children. *North Western Journal of Education*, 1896, *7*, 69–70.

31 Books on child study. *North Western Journal of Education*, 1896, *7*, 73–74.

32 Sense defects of school children: The eye and its actions. *North Western Journal of Education*, 1896, *7*, 99–100.

33 Lesson's in Tracy's "Psychology of Childhood." *North Western Journal of Education*, 1896, *7*, 102–103.

34 Tracy's "Psychology of Childhood." *North Western Journal of Education*, 1896, *7*, 134–135.

35 Sense defects of school children: Color blindness. *North Western Journal of Education*, 1896, *7*, 137–138.

36 Defects in hearing. *North Western Journal of Education*, 1896, *7*, 161–162.

37 Review of Wundt's "Grundriss der Psychologie." *Philosophical Review,* 1897, *6,* 76–81.

38 Intellectual philosophy. *North Western Journal of Education,* 1897, *7,* 230.

39 Nearsightedness in the school. *North Western Journal of Education,* 1897, *7,* 250–251.

40 Fatigue in children. *North Western Journal of Education,* 1897, *7,* 274–275.

41 Defects of sight. *North Western Monthly,* 1897, *8,* 35–39.

42 Heredity. *North Western Monthly,* 1897, *8,* 200–205.

43 Some effects of size on judgments of weight. *Psychological Review,* 1898, *5,* 25–54.

44 Pictures in the school room. *North Western Monthly,* 1898, *8,* 380.

45 The moral training of children. *North Western Monthly,* 1898, *8,* 431–435.

46 Some judgments on the size of familiar objects. *American Journal of Psychology,* 1898, *9,* 137–166.

47 Some questions in professional ethics. *Education,* 1899, *19,* 455–467.

48 Diversity in the high school. *Nebraska Teacher,* 1904, *6,* 412–414.

49 High school government. *Nebraska Teacher,* 1904, *7,* 76.

50 Let the university help. *Nebraska Teacher,* 1907, *10,* 103–104.

51 The theory of teaching. *Nebraska Teacher,* 1910, *12,* 124–126, 170–174, 240–242, 292–294, 334–335, 390–392, 430–432, 482–484. (Serial publication of eight lessons.)

52 Barnett's "Practical Pedagogy." *Nebraska Teacher,* 1910–1911, *13,* 120–121, 176–178, 238–240, 290–292, 338–340, 386–388, 434–436, 480–482. (Serial publication of eight lessons.)

53 The teacher and the school. *Nebraska Teacher,* 1911, *14,* 117–118, 170–172, 236–237, 298–300, 344–345, 392–393, 436–437, 492–494. (Serial publication of eight lessons.)

54 Personality and education. *Mid-West Quarterly,* 1918, *5,* 259–273.

55 On the estimation of the middle of lines. *American Journal of Psychology,* 1923, *34,* 313–358. (Completed before his death but published posthumously.)

Index